The Five Ways

The Five Ways

St. Thomas Aquinas' Proofs of God's Existence

ANTHONY KENNY

UNIVERSITY OF NOTRE DAME PRESS
Notre Dame, Indiana 46556

University of Notre Dame Press edition 1980
First published in 1969 by Routledge & Kegan Paul Ltd.
Reprinted by arrangement with Routledge & Kegan Paul Ltd.

Library of Congress Cataloging in Publication Data

Kenny, Anthony John Patrick.
    The five ways.

    Reprint of the 1969 ed. published by Routledge &
Kegan Paul Ltd. in series: Studies in ethics and the
philosophy of religion.
    Bibliography: p.
    1. God—Proof. 2. Thomas Aquinas, Saint, 1225?
–1274—Theology. I. Title.
[BT100.T4K46 1980]   231'.042   80-10416
ISBN 0-268-00952-X
ISBN 0-268-00950-3 pbk.

Manufactured in the United States of America

Contents

Preface

A draft of this book was delivered as a lecture course at Oxford in Michaelmas and Hilary Terms of the academic year 1967-8. A draft of chapter VI was read to a discussion group at Keele in 1968. I am grateful to the audiences on these occasions for their criticisms. I am indebted to Professor A. Flew, Mr. A. N. Prior, and Professor P. Geach for discussion and correspondence on particular points. I wish also to thank Miss P. Lloyd for typing the manuscript.

References to works of St. Thomas are given in abbreviated form as follows:

Summa Theologiae, without title. Part, question, article, reply; e.g. Ia 3, 2, ad 3.

Summa Contra Gentiles, ScG. Book, chapter: e.g. ScG. 1, 28.

Scriptum in IV Libros Sententiarium, *Sent*. Book, distinction, question, article, solution or *quaestiuncula*, reply; e.g. III Sent 25, 2, 3, ii ad 3.

Philosophical commentaries: On the *Metaphysics*, *In Meta*. Book, paragraph number of the Cathala edition: e.g. *In Meta* I, 47. On the *Physics*, *In Phys*. Book, paragraph number of the Maggiolo edition: e.g. *In Phys* I, 56. References to Aristotle give the Bekker pagination.

Quaestiones Disputatae: De Potentia, De Pot. De Veritate, De Ver. Quaestiones quodlibetales: Quodl.

I have tried to make the text intelligible to readers who know no Latin; but the original of any passage quoted will be found in the footnotes. The translation of St. Thomas is my own; but I have often been helped by using the Blackfriars translation of Fr. Timothy McDermott.

1

Introduction

The systematic study of proofs of God's existence is unfashionable among both philosophers and theologians. This book, therefore, will seem to many professional readers sadly anachronistic. To the lay reader, on the other hand, it will seem exasperatingly inconclusive. I shall not try to prove or disprove the existence of God; I should like to do one or the other, but I cannot do either. Instead I shall examine a single set of proofs, the Five Ways by which St. Thomas Aquinas, in the *Summa Theologiae*, said that the existence of God could be demonstrated. I shall attempt to establish what St. Thomas meant by the steps in these proofs, looking for illumination in parallel passages in his works, but not considering other independent proofs which he offers elsewhere. I shall then try to evaluate the arguments critically and show what in my opinion they establish and what they fail to establish. I shall not discuss how seriously St. Thomas meant the Five Ways as proofs. Some have suggested that they are arguments which he is quoting rather than using; others have said that they are not proofs at all, but rather ways of giving content to the notion of divinity. I myself think that St. Thomas meant them as seriously as he meant any other philosophical proof; but I shall not argue the point. I am interested in whether the arguments to be found in the *Summa Theologiae* do in fact constitute a rational proof of God's existence, rather than in whether St. Thomas himself thought they did or not.

There are many philosophers who are uninterested in proofs of God's existence because they believe the concept of *God* to be incoherent or empty of content. Reasons for thinking this were put forward some years ago by a number of contributors to the volume *New Essays in Philosophical Theology*. Some argued, on conventionalist grounds, that the notion of *necessary being* was self-contradictory; others argued, on verificationist grounds, that the proposition 'there is a God' was meaningless because unfalsifiable (Flew and Macintyre, 47ff, 96ff). Neither of these arguments seems to me effective against the type of natural theology attempted by Aquinas.

The conventionalist argument fails for two reasons. To say that God is a necessary being is not necessarily to say that 'God exists' is a necessary proposition: when Aquinas uses this description of God in the *Summa Theologiae* he means simply that God is imperishable. Moreover, it has not been shown that the necessity of necessarily true propositions derives from human convention; there is much evidence, in the recent history of philosophical logic, in the contrary direction. The notion of *necessary being*, therefore, has not been shown to be incoherent.[1]

The verificationist argument also fails. To ask of someone who believes that God made the universe 'what difference would it make in experience if God did not exist?' is like asking him 'what difference would it make in experience if the universe did not exist?' If there is a creator God, then of course 'God does not exist' is unfalsifiable; for if there were no God, on this hypothesis, there would be nobody to falsify anything. Verificationism itself is too much in need of qualification to be a useful tool against theism. We cannot restrict meaningful reference to the domain of the directly perceptible: there are too many counterexamples from the philosophy of science, the philosophy of mind, and the philosophy of perception itself. If we make our criteria more

[1] I have argued this at length in Williams and Montefiore, 131 ff.

generous and allow reference to entities whose effects are perceptible, then we do not *eo ipso* rule out meaningful reference to a God of whom the whole perceptible universe is alleged to be an effect. Of course, this causal relationship between God and the universe is itself problematic; but this problem is the ancient one, whether there is good reason to believe in a First Cause.

There are, of course, a number of traditional arguments against the existence of God, such as the problem of evil and the difficulty of reconciling human freedom with the divine omniscience and omnipotence. As commonly presented, they seem to me to contain a number of flaws. If they can be so amended as to constitute a valid disproof of God's existence, then of course the only interest in examining arguments in its favour lies in the detection of the fallacies they must contain. This may be of some philosophical importance, as is shown by the history of the ontological argument. Almost no one considers this argument valid, but hardly two people agree exactly where it goes wrong; and the discussion of it has frequently led to valuable philosophical insights.

It is not, in fact, very common for secular philosophers nowadays even to advance reasons for not considering arguments for the existence of God. Perhaps this is because Kant is credited with having done so once for all. Certainly Strawson must be a spokesman for the boredom of many when he says 'it is with very moderate enthusiasm that a twentieth century philosopher enters the field of philosophical theology, even to follow Kant's exposure of its illusions' (Strawson, 207). The criticisms of Kant are certainly still the most effective obstacle any rational theism has to meet; but they were directed at arguments rather different from the Five Ways and affect them, as will be seen, only obliquely.

The Five Ways fail, I shall argue, principally because it is much more difficult than at first appears to separate them from their background in medieval cosmology. Any

contemporary cosmological argument would have to be much
more different from the arguments of Aquinas than scholastic modernisations customarily are. A refutation of Kant's
criticisms would be a prolegomenon to such an argument;
but consideration of Kant is not essential to a critical analysis
of the medieval discussion.

Some theologians regard religion as a way of life which
can only be understood by participation and therefore cannot
be justified to an outsider on neutral rational grounds. Such
people must consider any attempt at a philosophical proof of
God's existence to be wrong-headed, and must find it inconceivable that such matters as whether everything in
motion has a mover could have any relevance to religion.
Formerly it was customary for Catholic theologians, following the First Vatican Council, to insist on the possibility of a
rational proof of theism, while Protestant theologians, starting from a conviction of the corruption of human nature,
regarded such proof as impossible, or at least impious. Now
it seems common for theologians in both traditions to adopt
a fideistic approach, to insist on commitment rather than
demonstration, and to accept the existence of a Creator, no
less than that of a Saviour, as a matter of faith. To me it
seems that if belief in the existence of God cannot be ration-
ally justified, there can be no good reason for adopting any
of the traditional monotheistic religions. A philosophical
proof of God's existence from the nature of the world would
not be the only form such a rational justification might take:
a man might, for instance, come to accept the existence of
God through believing something in the world to be a revelation from God; just as we might come to believe in the
existence of Martians by convincing ourselves that we were
intercepting messages from Mars. Whether such a conviction was rational would not depend, it seems to me, on
whether there was an independent proof of the existence of
the beings in question in each case. But a valid philosophical
proof of God's existence would be a sufficient, though not a
necessary, condition for the possibility of a rational accept-

ance of theism. Those philosophers and theologians who still consider belief in God to need rational justification frequently offer the arguments of Aquinas as such a justification. Anyone who shares their interest in religion and their concern for rationality has good reason to examine the Five Ways with care.

2

The First Way

The first and most obvious way is based on motion. It is certain as a matter of sense-observation that some things in this world are in motion. Now whatever is in motion, is moved by something else. For nothing is in motion except in so far as it is in potentiality to the term of its motion. Something moves, on the other hand, in so far as it is in actuality. This is because to move is precisely to bring something from potentiality to actuality; but a thing cannot be brought from potentiality to actuality except by something which is itself in actuality. Thus, something which is actually hot, like fire, makes something which is potentially hot — say wood — to be actually hot: and in this way it moves and alters it. Now it is not possible for the same thing to be, at the same time and in the same respect, in actuality and in potentiality; for what is actually hot cannot simultaneously be potentially hot, though it may simultaneously be potentially cold. So it is impossible that in the same respect and in the same manner anything should be both mover and moved, or that it should move itself. So whatever is in motion, must be moved by something else. Moreover, this something else, if it too is in motion, must itself be moved by something else, and that in turn by yet another thing. But this cannot go on for ever: because if it did there would be no first mover, and consequently no other mover at all, since second movers do not move except when moved by a first mover, just as a stick does not move anything except when moved by a hand. And so we must reach a first mover which is not moved by anything: and this all men think of as God.[1] (Ia, 2, 2.)

The First Way is based on *motus*. I have translated St. Thomas' term by 'motion': but from the text itself it is clear that the Latin word has a wider meaning than the English one, since the example given of *motus* is the action of fire on wood. 'Change' is perhaps the English word whose natural sense is nearest. Following Aristotle, (*Physics* E, 226a 23ff) St. Thomas distinguished three kinds of *motus*: change of quality, change of quantity and change of place. The first is exemplified when a hot body becomes cold, or a white surface becomes black; it is called technically 'alteration'. The second is increase or decrease in size. The third is called by St. Thomas 'local motion': it is the only one which would naturally be called 'motion' in English.

[1] *Responsio:* Dicendum quod Deum esse quinque viis probari potest.
Prima autem et manifestior via est quae sumitur ex parte motus. Certum est enim et sensu constat aliqua moveri in hoc mundo. Omne autem quod movetur ab alio movetur. Nihil enim movetur nisi secundum quod est in potentia ad illud ad quod movetur. Movet autem aliquid secundum quod est actu; movere enim nihil aliud est quam educere aliquid de potentia in actum, de potentia autem non potest aliquid reduci in actum nisi per aliquid ens actu: sicut calidum in actu ut ignis facit lignum quod est calidum in potentia esse calidum in actu et per hoc movet et alterat ipsum. Non autem est possible quod idem sit simul in actu et in potentia secundum idem sed solum secundum diversa: quod enim est calidum in actu non potest simul esse calidum in potentia sed est simul frigidum in potentia. Impossible est ergo quod idem et eodem motu aliquid sit movens et motum vel quod moveat seipsum. Oportet ergo omne quod movetur ab alio moveri. Si ergo id a quo movetur moveatur, oportet et ipsum ab alio moveri, et illud ab alio. Hoc autem non est procedere in infinitum, quia sic non esset aliquod primum movens et per consequens nec aliquod aliud movens, quia moventia secunda non movent nisi per hoc quod sunt mota a primo movente, sicut baculus non movet nisi per hoc quod est motus a manu. Ergo necesse est devenire ad aliquod primum movens quod a nullo movetur, et hoc omnes intelligunt Deum.

However, though the sense of '*motus*' is wider than that of 'motion' it is not quite as wide as that of 'change'. A change of some kind, we might say, has taken place whenever some significantly tensed proposition changes from being true to being false or from being false to being true. On this account, the assassination of Caesar, Anselm's inventing an ontological argument, and Adam's being outgrown by Cain are all changes; because with the events in question the following propositions ceased to be false and became true: 'Caesar has been assassinated', 'Anselm has hit upon an ontological argument', 'Adam has been outgrown by Cain'. But none of these events would strictly be called '*motus*' by Aquinas. Caesar's death was not a change in a substance, but the destruction of a substance: it may be called '*mutatio*' but not '*motus*' (*In Physic* V, II, 658). Anselm's invention of his argument was a mental, not a corporeal event; and mental events are only *motus* in an improper, Platonic, sense (ScG I, 13 *sciendum autem*). Adam's being outgrown by Cain is a change in the relationship between Adam and Cain; but the only *motus* involved is the increase in size of Cain; Adam is not thereby 'in motion' (*In Physic* V, III, 667).

For this reason I have retained the traditional translations 'motion' and 'move' for '*motus*' and '*movere*'. I have also, in translation, made a distinction between two different uses of the passive form '*moveri*'. 'Move' in English may be transitive or intransitive; I may move someone out of my way, or move out of his way. To express the intransitive sense of 'move' in Latin, one simply uses the passive mood of the transitive verb. There is thus no simple way of distinguishing in Latin between 'it is moving' (intransitive) and 'it is being moved'. This small point is not trivial, as we shall see: there is reason to believe that St. Thomas was misled, at a crucial point in his argument, by the double sense of the Latin '*movetur*'. In order to avoid begging any questions, I have translated '*movetur*', when used absolutely, by 'is in motion', and when used with a complement, by 'is (being) moved by'. I have avoided the intransitive use of 'move' and use the verb only when an object could be supplied, as in 'I moved my belongings'. Similarly I distinguish between 'motion' and 'movement', reserving the latter for the active sense, as in 'my movement of my belongings'. This will purchase clarity at the cost of occasional artificiality.

After these preambles, we can ask what is meant by the first step in the argument: 'It is certain as a matter of sense-observation that some things in this world are in motion'. There is a dispute among scholastic commentators whether St. Thomas has in mind physical or metaphysical motion (see, for instance, Masi, p. 15). The sense of the dispute is not entirely clear. In a parallel passage of the *Summa contra Gentiles* (ScG I, 13) St. Thomas states the premiss thus: 'It is obvious to the senses that some things are in motion, for instance the sun.'[1] The example is unfortunately geocentric; but clearly the argument would not be affected if we altered the last phrase to 'for instance the moon'. The example of *motus* is obviously meant to be a case of local motion from place to place. That St. Thomas is not thinking *only* of local motion is shown by the example of heating in the *Summa Theologiae*. But both examples are instances of motion as defined in the *Physics*, and therefore, presumably, of 'physical motion'. What could be meant by saying that the argument is based not on physical, but metaphysical motion?

Four ways of understanding this theory are possible.

(i) St. Thomas — it may be said — is thinking not only of local motion and change in size and sensible qualities, but also of mental events and processes. Such changes were called by some scholastics '*motus metaphysici*'. This interpretation might seem to be supported by the fact that in the *contra Gentiles* teaching is given as an example of moving (ScG I, 13 *si autem praedicta*). But though teaching can be done only by beings with minds, it is not itself a purely mental process. Thinking, which is such a process, is sometimes described by St. Thomas as a motion in this broad

---

[1] Patet autem sensu aliquid moveri, ut puta solem.

sense: to think of an object is to be moved by that object
(1a, 18, 3 ad 1). But this cannot be what St. Thomas has
in mind in the First Way. For of this sort of motion it is not
true that nothing can move itself. For a man can think of
himself; therefore, if to think of A is to be moved by A, a
man can move himself (ScG I, 13, *sciendum autem quod
Plato*). But this would wreck the argument to the Unmoved
Mover.

(ii) It is possible to take '*motus metaphysici*' to include the
creation and annihilation of substances (e.g. Salamucha p.
346). But that would make the First Way question —
begging.

(iii) The thesis may mean that the First Way depends
upon a particular metaphysical analysis of motion rather
than on any theory which a physicist might put forward
about it. So understood, the thesis is true: the metaphysical
analysis of motion in terms of actuality and potentiality is an
essential step in St. Thomas' reasoning. But on this interpretation the thesis is irrelevant to the understanding of the
first premise of the argument. The question here is: which
are the phenomena to which this metaphysical analysis is to
be applied?

(iv) The thesis may mean that the phenomena in question
are phenomena of an exclusively metaphysical kind: transitions from potentiality to actuality detectible only by the
spiritual eye of the metaphysician. So understood, the thesis
seems nonsensical in itself, and false as an interpretation of
St. Thomas. His examples are of perfectly ordinary motions
which appear, as he says, obvious to the senses. His argument would never have been interpreted in terms of metaphysical motions, one feels, had the interpreters not feared
that the First Way, understood in terms of visible changes,
had been undermined by Newton's laws of motion. We shall
have to consider later whether this fear is well grounded;
we can see already that the appeal to metaphysical motions
is a poor way to assuage it. For it preserves the argument of
the First Way from criticism only by making its first premise
disputable. If that premise states that there take place occult

metaphysical transitions, one may take leave to doubt it. If it simply states that in the world some things are in motion from place to place, others grow and shrink and others get hotter and colder, then the First Way commences at least with an unimpeachable truth. It is in this sense that I shall understand it.[1]

In the *Summa contra Gentiles* the First Way is stated at much greater length than in the *Summa Theologiae*. Moreover the argument is explicitly attributed to Aristotle.[2] It begins as follows. 'Whatever is in motion, is moved by something else. Now it is obvious to the senses that some things are in motion, for instance the sun. Any such things therefore is moved by some other mover. This mover in turn either is in motion or is not in motion. If it is not in motion, then the thesis is proved that it is necessary to assign some immovable mover. And this we call God. If, however, it is in motion, then it is moved by another mover. Either this regress must go on for ever; or we must come to some immovable mover. But the regress cannot go on for ever. Therefore it is necessary to assign some immovable first mover.'[3]

---

[1] Owens (2), pp. 116–121, 212, etc. argues that the First Way 'unlike the Aristotelian argument from motion, proceeds from sensible change analysed ultimately in terms of existential act'. By the 'existential act' (*esse*) of a motion he appears to mean the actual occurrence of a motion, this being taken to be something different from the motion occurring (p. 105). But the texts he quotes from St. Thomas do not seem to support the nonsensical view that when you have explained a particular motion at a particular time you have to explain also the occurrence of that motion.

[2] In fact the First Way in the *Contra Gentiles* uses a patchwork of Aristotelian passages drawn from two separate arguments, in the Seventh and Eighth books of the *Physics*, which conclude not to the existence of God but to the presence of a soul in the outermost sphere of the heavens. For the details of St. Thomas' adaptation of Aristotle, see Owens (2).

[3] Omne quod movetur, ab alio movetur. Patet autem sensu, aliquid moveri, ut puta solem. Ergo alio movente movetur. Aut ergo illud movens movetur, aut non. Si non movetur, ergo habemus propositum,

In this proof, as Aquinas goes on to say, two propositions in particular need to be established. The first is that whatever is in motion is moved by something else; the second is that it is impossible to go on for ever in the series of moved and moving objects.

The sense of the first dictum is not clear. 'Whatever is in motion is moved by something else'. Does this mean that whatever is now in motion is *now being moved* by something else? Or does it mean that whatever is in motion has, *at some time or other*, been moved by something else? That is to say, how seriously are we to take the present tense of the verb *movetur*, which can mean either 'is being moved' or 'is (at some time or other) moved'? If we take the former interpretation, then the series of moved movers which Aquinas goes on to discuss will be a series of simultaneous movers; if the latter, then it may be a series stretching backwards in time.

Clearly, the principle makes a weaker, and more plausible, claim on the second interpretation than it does on the first. Following a long line of commentators, let us consider a stationary billiard ball. It does seem true that this will not move unless it is moved by something else, e.g. by another billiard ball. And it will not be moved by a stationary billiard ball, but only by a rolling one; and any such second billiard ball will be a mover in motion. But the motion of the second billiard ball need not be simultaneous with the motion of the first: the second may come to rest long before the first has stopped rolling. So the series of moving and moved billiard balls may be a series reaching backwards in time. It cannot be such a series which Aquinas has in mind in the First Way. For he did not think that there was anything inconceivable in an endless series of temporally ordered causes: he expressly said that there was nothing impossible in the

---

quod necesse est ponere aliquod movens immobile. Et hoc dicimus Deum. Si autem movetur, ergo ab alio movente movetur. Aut ergo est procedere in infinitum: aut est devenire ad aliquod movens immobile. Sed non est procedere in infinitum. Ergo necesse est ponere aliquod primum movens immobile.

idea of one man being begotten by another, and the other by a third, and so on ad infinitum (Ia 46 2 ad 7). It cannot, then, be a regress of such causes which the First Way declares impossible.

It seems, then, that we must take the principle as meaning that everything in motion is being moved by something simultaneously in motion. This is suggested by St. Thomas' own example of a series of movers (a hand moving a stick which is moving a stone) and by a passage in *Physics* 4 (242a 58), quoted by St. Thomas (ScG I, 13 *Quarum prima*) in which Aristotle says explicitly that the motion of what is moved and the motion of its mover must be simultaneous. But two great difficulties at once present themselves. First, so understood, the principle seems to admit of obvious counterexamples. I myself, as I type; the dog running in the field outside; the weeds pushing through the pavement; the apple falling from the tree; the croquet ball passing through the hoop: all these seem to be examples of things in motion which are not being moved by anything. Secondly, if 'is moved' means 'is being moved', then a being which is not moved is simply something which is, at the present moment, at rest. So understood, an unmoved mover is not necessarily an entity which throughout its whole history remains unmoved; still less is it something, as St. Thomas rather cavalierly says, 'immovable'. Taken this way the First Way will not lead us to an unmoved mover we can call God; it will not lead us beyond a stationary billiard ball.

To the first of these difficulties St. Thomas has an answer. It can best be seen by following the second of the three arguments which he borrows from Aristotle in favour of his principle. This is a proof by cases that everything which is in motion is moved by something else (ScG I, 13 *Secundo probat*; *Phys* 7, 254b 6ff; *In Physic*, VIII, 102ff).

Motion, says St. Thomas, may be subdivided into motion *per accidens*, and motion *per se*. If something is in motion because it is located in something else, then its motion is *per accidens*; a sleeping man in a travelling ship is in motion *per accidens*. A thing is also in motion *per accidens* if a part of it is in motion: a man waving his hands is in motion *per accidens*.[1] Motion *per se* is defined as motion which is not *per accidens*. Now it is obvious, St. Thomas says, that whatever is in motion *per accidens* is not moved by itself; for it is moved at the motion of something else. This seems plausible in the case of the man asleep in the boat: but what of me, sitting at my typewriter? This too is motion *per accidens*, according to St. Thomas; I am in motion because of the motion of my fingers, which are a part of me. But though I may be said to be in motion *because of* the motion of my fingers, I can hardly be said to be moved *by* the motion of my fingers. On the other hand my fingers are certainly moved by me; so that if we waive the oddness of saying that I am moved by my fingers, we have to say my fingers move me and I move my fingers. In that case, the relation of *moving* cannot be an asymmetrical relation; which it has to be if St. Thomas is ever to base an infinite regress upon it. So it appears that this type of motion *per accidens* either provides a counterexample to the principle that whatever is in motion is moved by something else or else renders the principle useless for the purposes of the First Way.

Suppose that I move, not just my fingers, but my whole body. Is this motion *per se*, or *per accidens*? Here the argument in the *contra Gentiles* parts company with the passage in the *Physics* on which it is based. Aristotle here allows that animals are moved by themselves, and he states his general conclusion as 'everything in motion is moved by something', not 'everything in motion is moved by something else' (254b 25). Aquinas does not agree that animals are moved 'by themselves' (*a se*); he admits only that they are in motion 'of themselves' (*ex se*). He explains this by saying that animals are moved by *their souls*. There is no mention of souls in the *Physics* passage. Aristotle says that the whole animal moves itself, and that its body may be

---

[1] St. Thomas gives a third, untranslatable, example. If we were accustomed to say that a man's disease is in motion when the man himself is on his way to hospital, this would provide an example of the third sort of motion *per accidens* which he has in mind.

moved naturally or unnaturally depending on the kind of motion and the kind of stuff it is made of.[1] He says that in animals there must be something that moves and something that is moved, as in ships and artefacts, but that it is not clear exactly what it is that moves. It is not clear to me even what kind of thing Aristotle was hesitating about: was he thinking of the soul or of a part of the body such as the heart?

Aquinas, at any rate, clearly opted for saying that an animal was moved by his soul. This prevents his maxim from being refuted by the example of a running or growing animal. It does so by making the motion of an animal no longer a case of *per se* motion. For if an animal has two parts, body and soul, then any locomotion or growth of the animal's body will be only a *per accidens* motion of the whole animal, like any movement of my fingers at the typewriter. Such *per accidens* motion, we have seen, need not be an asymmetrical relationship. But this need no longer embarrass Aquinas. For he can say that *per se* my fingers are moved not by me but by my soul; and this *per se* relationship *is* asymmetrical, since my fingers do not move my soul. Fortunately, we need not here inquire whether this concept of the soul as a mover is a coherent one. It is sufficient to note that the dictum 'whatever is in motion is moved by something else' will not lead us to God as a conclusion. The Aristotelian soul of any animal or plant will be an unmoved mover in the required sense.

Per se motion, as we have seen, is divided by Aristotle into natural motion and unnatural ('violent') motion. Besides the characteristic motions of animals, the fall of heavy bodies and the rise of volatile substances provide examples of natural motion. The classic instance of unnatural motion is the rise of a heavy projectile: the horizontal motion of a croquet ball would also serve as an example. Both Aristotle and St. Thomas say that it is obvious that

[1] He is presumably thinking of the contrast between (*a*) an elephant walking with the gait proper to elephants, (*b*) an elephant falling from a cliff because it is a heavy body, (*c*) an elephant being dragged uphill by a rope.

something in unnatural motion is moved by something else. It is, we have agreed, obvious that a heavy stone will not rise unless something throws it, and that a croquet ball does not travel through a hoop unless someone hits it; but it is not at all obvious that the rising stone and the rolling croquet ball are, at all times of their motion, still being moved by some other body. In the last chapter of the *Physics* ((4), 266b 27) Aristotle insists that despite the appearances this is in fact the case. A thrower, he explains, imparts motion not only to a projectile, but also to the medium (e.g. air) through which the projectile is thrown; and in addition he imparts to the medium a quasi-magnetic power of moving the projectile. When the thrower ceases moving, the air ceases to be itself in motion — otherwise the same problem would arise for the continuing motion of the air as arises for the continuing motion of the projectile — but it does not cease to possess and exercise the power to move the projectile.

St. Thomas, in his commentary on this chapter, accepted Aristotle's view and rejected the impetus theory of some of his contemporaries, according to which the power of moving was communicated not to the medium surrounding the projectile but to the projectile itself. The Aristotelian theory is obviously open to Newtonian objections; but it does, in the case of projectiles, preserve the principle 'whatever is in motion is being moved by something else'. The projectile is being moved by air; the air, not being in motion, needs no mover. But once again it does so only by making the regress argument of the First Way impotent to prove the existence of God. For the air surrounding a projectile is, on this view, a perfectly good unmoved mover.

The most testing case for the principle, Aristotle thought, was the case of the natural movements of lifeless bodies. The fall of a stone is undoubtedly a case of motion; yet a falling stone has no obvious mover.[1] We cannot say it moves itself:

---

[1] In this case Newtonian mechanics, explaining the fall by the gravitational pull of the earth, would seem to be more favourable to Aristotle's principle than his own mechanics are.

only living things do that, and if a stone could move itself at all, it could stop itself and move itself in various directions (*Physics* 4 255a 5ff). None the less, Aristotle says, there are two ways in which heavy and light bodies owe their motion to a moving agent. First, they rise and fall because that is their nature, and so they owe their motion to whatever gave them their nature; they are moved, he says, by their 'generator'. Thus, when fire heats water, a heavy substance, it turns it into steam, which is light, and being light, naturally rises; and thus the fire is the cause of the natural motion of the steam and can be said to move it. The steam, however, might be prevented from rising by an obstacle — e.g. by the lid of a kettle. In such a case, some agent might allow the steam to rise by removing the lid of the kettle. Such an agent would also be a mover; and this is the second way in which Aristotle thinks natural motions are due to movers. Such a mover is a *removens prohibens*, the remover of an obstacle.[1]

Once we count generators or obstacle-removers as moving agents, it is clear that we can no longer preserve the principle 'whatever is in motion is being moved by another'. The examples given above do not refute the principle, since the action of the agents would be more or less simultaneous with their effects. However, if someone pulls out a bathplug the water may continue to flow downwards long after he has gone away, and if we ask for the generating cause of the heaviness of a falling boulder we may not find one later than the cooling of the earth's crust. So that when Aquinas, following Aristotle, says that things which move naturally, such as heavy and light objects, are moved by their generators and by the removers of obstacles, he must mean that they are being *or have been* moved; and this will not contribute to any simultaneous infinite regress.

Some Thomists claim that the crucial fact which the First Way seeks to explain is not the tendency which a heavy body has to fall — this, they admit, is something which was given

---

[1] Aristotle's own example is somebody removing a pillar and causing the fall of whatever the pillar supported.

to the heavy body by whatever it was in the past which made it heavy — but rather the current exercise of that tendency in actual motion. Every such potentiality of a creature, they say, needs to be actualized by the immediate action of the Creator.[1] This seems to be a piece of nonsense. To say that something has a tendency to move is precisely to say that unless something interferes, it will move; if it moves therefore, when interference is removed, no further explanation of its motion is called for apart from the tendency and the removal of the interference. This appears to be what Thomas himself thought when he wrote his commentary on Aristotle's *Physics*. Commenting on the eighth book he says: 'Some people inquire why heavy and light objects are moved to their appropriate place. The cause of this is that they have a natural tendency to their places. This is what being light is, to have a tendency to be high up; and this is the meaning of 'heavy', namely having a tendency to be low down. So to ask why a heavy body moves downward is simply to ask why it is heavy. And so the very same thing which makes it heavy, causes its downward motion.'[2]

So far we have been considering just one of the arguments for the principle that whatever is in motion is moved by something else, namely Aristotle's proof by cases. St. Thomas reproduces two other Aristotelian arguments for the principle. Both of them purport to be refutations of the idea that something might move itself. Even if successful, such a refutation seems to leave something further needing proof. If a thing cannot be moved by itself, it does not follow

[1] Cf. Masi p. 25 and the passage from Owens (1) cited in note to p. 11 above.

[2] Licet enim actus levis sit esse sursum, tamen a quibusdam quaeritur quare gravia et levia moventur in propria loca. Sed causa huius est, quia habent naturalem aptitudinem ad talia loca. Hoc enim est esse leve, habere apititudinem ad hoc quod sit sursum: et haec est etiam ratio gravis, habere aptitudinem ad hoc quod sit deorsum. Unde nihil est aliud quaerere quare grave movetur deorsum, quam quaerere quare est grave. Et sic illud idem quod facit ipsum grave, facit ipsum moveri deorsum (*In Physic*, VIII, 8, 1034).

that it must be moved by something else. Why cannot it just be in motion, without *being moved* by anything, whether by itself or by anything else? Does not the argument need completing with a proof that whatever is in motion is being moved? Perhaps St. Thomas missed this because of the double sense of the Latin *movetur*, which we have seen has to do duty both for 'is in motion' and 'is being moved'. But in any case, the two arguments against self-movement are fallacious.

The first argument is a *reductio ad absurdum* (*Phys.* H, 241b 35–6; *ScG* I 13 *Quorum primum*). A self-moving object must (*a*) have parts, in order to be in motion at all; (*b*) be in motion as a whole, and not just in one of its parts; and (*c*) originate its own motion. But this is impossible. From (*b*) it follows that if any part of the body is at rest, the whole of it is at rest. But if the whole body's being at rest depends upon a part's being at rest, then the motion of the whole body depends upon the motion of the part; and thus it does not originate its own motion. 'So that which was supposed to be moved by itself is not moved by itself'.

This argument is vitiated by a double equivocation in the expression '*sequitur ad*' which I have translated as 'depends upon'. First, it equivocates between logical and causal dependence, as Sir David Ross points out in his commentary on *Physics* 242a 38: 'the motion of the whole logically implies the motion of the part, but is not necessarily causally dependent on it'. (Ross, p. 669). Secondly, it equivocates between being a necessary condition and being a sufficient condition. The part's being at rest is a sufficient condition for the whole's being at rest; from this it follows only that the motion of the part is a necessary condition for the motion of the whole, and not that it is a sufficient condition for it. Hence the argument in no way proves that something else, namely the motion of the part, is a causally sufficient condition for the motion of the alleged self-mover. So the *reductio ad absurdum* fails: it has not been shown that there cannot be a body which can initiate its own movement without external causal concurrence.

The second proof that nothing can move itself is the one taken most seriously by contemporary Thomists, and is the only one used in the *Summa Theologiae*. It makes use of the notions of actuality and potentiality,[1] which may be briefly explained as follows. A pint of water can become steam, a pale man can get sunburnt, a small bush can grow six feet high. In such cases medieval Aristoteleans would say that the stuff is actually water, but is potentially steam; that the man is actually pale but potentially brown; the bush is actually small but potentially tall. Or, to put it another way, the substance has the actuality of being water, the potentiality of being steam; the man has the actuality of being pale, the potentiality of being brown; the bush has the actuality of smallness but the potentiality of tallness. Any change of motion is a passage from potentiality to actuality: the growth of the bush is its passage from being potentially tall to being actually tall; and as long as it is still growing it is still in a state of potentiality towards tallness: until it is finished growing it is not yet as tall as it can be and will be.

It is against the background of this theory that St. Thomas presents his argument. In its briefer form, in the *contra Gentiles*, it runs as follows: 'Nothing is simultaneously in actuality and in potentiality in the same respect. But everything which is in motion is, as such, in potentiality . . . Now everything which is moving is as such, in actuality; because nothing acts except when it is in actuality. Therefore nothing is, with respect to the same motion, both mover and moved. And so nothing moves itself.'[2]

With a certain qualification, the first premise is true. Nothing can be both actually F and potentially F, since 'A

---

[1] I use these ugly terms instead of 'act' and 'potency' because 'act' is needed in too many other senses, and because it helps to have a pair of obviously technical terms.

[2] Nihil idem est simul actu et potentia respectu eiusdem. Sed omne quod movetur, inquantum huiusmodi, est in potentia . . . Omne autem quod movet est in actu, inquantum huiusmodi: quia nihil agit nisi secundum est in actu. Ergo nihil est respectu eiusdem motus movens et motum. Et sic nihil movet seipsum (ScG I, 13, *Tertio probat*).

is potentially F' means 'A can be F but is not actually F'. The qualification is that 'F' must be a predicate which does not admit of degrees. The bush cannot be both actually and potentially six feet high; it either is or is not six feet high. But it can be both actually and potentially tall in the sense that it can be already tall but have the power of growing taller. 'Tall' unlike 'six feet high' admits of degrees: a thing can be more or less tall.

The second premise is also true. If something is changing, then it has not yet finished changing; and if it has not yet finished changing it is going to change further. If it is in fact going to change further then it now can change further: what a thing will do, that it can do. Therefore whatever is now changing has the potentiality for further change in one sense of the word 'potentiality'.[1] But again we must bear in mind the qualification made above: that a thing is growing taller doesn't mean that it is not already tall.

The third premise is the crucial one. In the *Summa Theologiae* it is argued for as follows: 'To move is precisely to bring something from potentiality to actuality; but a thing cannot be brought from potentiality to actuality except by something which is itself in actuality. Thus, something which is actually hot, like fire, makes something which is potentially hot — say wood — to be actually hot.'[2] The principle that only what is actually F will make something else become F does not seem universally true: a kingmaker need not himself be king, and it is not dead men who commit murders. Still, there are many everyday examples to support it: only what is hot will heat you, and it is no good trying to dry yourself with a wet towel. Moreover, the properties of hotness and coldness and wetness and dryness play a crucial part in St. Thomas' physics. For they meet, according to Aristotelian theory, in binary combinations in the four elements, water being wet and cold, fire hot and dry, and so on. And from earth, air, fire and water all else is made.

[1] For other possible senses, see below p. 60.
[2] For the Latin text, see p. 7 above.

There is a difficulty that 'hot', 'wet' and so on are all vague predicates like 'tall': something which is hot *may* cool you if it is not as hot as you are. Still, it would not be difficult to overcome this objection by rephrasing the principle: 'A can make B become F-er, only if A is itself F-er than B'. Then, unfortunately, it will no longer be true that nothing is both moving and moved in the same respect. For the kettle may be getting hotter while making the water hotter. But so qualified the principle will fit pretty well the phenomena of the conduction of heat.

The real difficulty is that heat does not arise only by conduction. Of course St. Thomas could not know about electric heaters; but even in the thirteenth century it was possible to start a fire by rubbing two sticks together. This objection might be met by saying that the phenomenon merely proves the presence of the element, fire, in the constitution of the stick. But if so, then it seems that the element can be present without being actually hot, and Aquinas' principle is still falsified.

Moreover, it is hard to see how the principle is supposed to apply in the case of local motion. In local motion from A to B a body which was potentially at B becomes actually at B. Is St. Thomas saying that a body can be moved to B only by something which is already at B? In the case of projectiles, this is actually the case according to Aristotelean theory; the medium through which the projectile travels, which on that theory is what actually moves the projectile, does reach as far as the end point of the projectile's travel. But in all the other cases of motion which Aquinas considered—the movement of an animal by its soul, the movement of a light body by the agent which made it light, the movement of a heavy body caused by an agent who moves its support—the principle seems to be false, even according to his own account of the matter. Applied to change in size, the principle seems even more inapplicable. A man who fattens oxen need not himself be fat.

The falsifications of the principle are fatal to the argument. For unless the principle is true, the conclusion contradicting

the possibility of a self-mover does not follow. If something
can be made F by an agent which is merely potentially F,
there seems no reason why something should not actualize
its own potentiality to F-ness.

But suppose the conclusion were sound, and such self-
movement was impossible. It would still be impossible for
Aquinas to go on to prove, by the infinite regress argument,
that there exists an unmoved mover at all resembling God.
For the conclusion establishes, at most, that nothing is both
mover and moved *in the same respect* (e.g. in temperature).
But if the final conclusion is to reach God, 'unmoved' must
mean changing *in no respect*. For all the regress argument
shows, however, the cause of all local motion might be a
stationary object which changed its temperature; and the
cause of all change in temperature might be an object of
constant heat which moved from place to place. Indeed, the
regress argument will not take us even this far. For even if
it is true that what heats must be hot, this in no way implies
that it has not itself *become* hot. At most, then, an 'unmoved
mover' with respect to heat would be a body whose temperature is at this moment constant. But even this, of course,
has not been shown: it has not been shown, for instance, that
a body A cannot heat a body B while itself *losing* heat and
thus changing its temperature. Even if it be said that on
Aristotelean principles this could not be the case unless
some further body C were communicating coldness to B,
there would still be neither an infinite regress (nothing
beyond A is heating B) nor an unmoved mover (A is not
unmoved in respect of temperature).

So much then, for the main element of the first part of the
First Way, the principle that whatever is in motion is moved
by something else.

The second part of the First Way consists in the proof
that it is impossible to go on for ever in a series of things
moved and moving. If it is true that when A is in motion
there must be some B which moves A, then if B is itself in
motion there must be some C moving B and so on. This,

Aquinas says, cannot go on for ever and so we must come to some X which moves without being in motion.

Why cannot the series go on for ever? In the *Summa contra Gentiles*, Aquinas quotes three arguments from Aristotle.

The first of these comes from the seventh book of the *Physics* (H 241b). It depends on the premise that whatever is in motion is a body. 'Every body which moves in motion is moved at the same time as it moves' says Aquinas; and in Aristotle's text this is supported by a cryptic argument, which is thus expounded by Ross (p. 669). A's movement of B is simultaneous with B's motion. A's movement of B is simultaneous with A's motion. Therefore, A's motion is simultaneous with B's motion. The conclusion follows in virtue of the unexceptionable principle that two things which are simultaneous with a third thing are themselves simultaneous. The first premise, however, seems suspicious. A's movement of B is certainly simultaneous with B's movement by A since they are one and the same event. Since we supposed that the mover moves in motion, necessarily the motion of the mover and the movement of the moved are simultaneous; for the mover moves at the same time as the moved is moved. But is B's movement by A simultaneous with B's motion? No proof is given, and one suspects that neither Aristotle nor Aquinas realised that one was necessary, being misled by the fact that the same Greek and Latin word has to mean both 'is in motion' and 'is being moved'.[1] The second premise, considered as a general thesis about movement, seems equally gratuitous. At best it functions as a restriction of the scope of the regress argument to those movers which move when and only when they are in motion.

The argument continues as follows. If, wherever you have a series of moved movers, the motion of the moving body is simultaneous with the motion of the moved body, then if you have an infinite series of moved movers, you have an infinite number of bodies in motion whenever one

[1] See above p. 8.

of the series is in motion. 'But any one of them, being finite, is in motion for a finite time. Therefore all these infinite bodies are in motion for a finite time. But this is impossible.'[1]

What is wrong, we might ask, with an infinite number of bodies being in motion for a finite time? 'An infinite motion in a finite time' sounds shocking; but only because there seems something odd in a body's travelling an infinite distance in a finite time. But why should not an infinite number of bodies each travel a finite distance in a finite time?

Well, says Aristotle (H, 242b 45ff), add together all the finite distances, travelled by the infinite number of bodies, and you will get an infinite distance which cannot be traversed in a finite time. But, we might retort, there is no single thing which travels an infinite distance, only many things travelling a finite distance. Not so, he retorts (242b 59ff); one body can move another only if it is in contact with it; so all these contiguous moving and moved bodies make up one large body (which need not be infinite). And *this* body will have to travel an infinite distance in a finite time; which is impossible.

This argument, which is partially reproduced by St. Thomas, seems to fail partly because it is not the case that if a body has parts each of which travels a certain distance then the body as a whole travels the sum of those distances. Moreover, if, as Aristotle argues, an infinite number of bodies added together may make a merely finite body, why should not an infinite number of journeys added together make a merely finite journey?

The second argument of the *contra Gentiles* comes from the eighth book of the *Physics* (256a 13ff) and is the only one reproduced in the *Summa Theologiae*. Take an ordered series of moving and moved objects such that each in turn is moved by another. 'If the first mover is removed or ceases from

---

[1] Omnia ista infinita simul moventur dum unum eorum movetur. Sed unum eorum, cum sit finitum, movetur tempore finito. Ergo omnia illa infinita moventur tempore finito. Hoc autem est impossible (ScG I, 13, *Quarum prima*).

moving, none of the others will move or be moved; because the first is the cause of the movement of all the others.'[1] For 'second movers move only when moved by a first mover, as a stick does not move unless moved by a hand'.[2] 'But' the argument concludes 'if there is an infinite series of movers and moved, there will be no first mover, but all will be as it were intermediate movers'.[3]

In this argument there is an equivocation in the word 'first', noticed by the sixteenth-century commentator Cajetan. 'An intermediate cause' writes Cajetan 'as such needs only to be a middle causal link between an earlier cause and its effect; therefore an intermediate cause as such needs to be dependent not on a first cause, but on an earlier cause.'[4] In the first step of the argument above, the word 'first' could be replaced by the word 'earlier', used in a non-temporal sense. This is shown by the very example given, since a hand would not be, according to St. Thomas, a first cause. Whereas in the second step of the argument, 'first mover' must mean 'mover preceded by no earlier mover'; otherwise there would be no reason to say that in an infinite series there will be no first mover. But if the word 'first' is

---

[1] In moventibus et motis ordinatis, quorum scilicet unum per ordinem ab alio movetur, hoc necesse est inveniri, quod, remoto primo movente vel cessante a motione, nullum aliorum movebit neque movebitur: quia primum est causa movendi omnibus aliis (ScG I, 13, *secunda ratio*).

[2] Moventia secunda non movent nisi per hoc quod sunt mota a primo movente, sicut baculus non movet nisi per hoc quod est motus a manu (Ia, 2, 3, c).

[3] Si sint moventia et mota per ordinem in infinitum, non erit aliquod primum movens, sed omnia erunt quasi media moventia (ScG I, 13, *secunda ratio*).

[4] Causa media ut sic, nihil aliud exiget quam ut in causando mediet: sed hoc, scilicet in causando mediare, sufficienter salvatur, si inter aliquam priorem causam et effectum aliqua media causalitatis sit: ergo media causa ex ratione qua media causa, non exigit dependentiam a prima causa, sed a priore. (The commentary is printed beneath the text of the Leonine edition of the *Summa Theologiae*, Ia, 2, 3c.) For a modern version of Cajetan's criticism see Williams.

taken in this sense in the first step of the argument, then that step assumes what the argument is to prove, namely that every ordered series of movers has a first term.

Aquinas' third proof runs as follows: 'That which moves as instrument cannot move unless there is something which moves as principal. But if there is an infinite series of things moving and moved, then all will be as it were instrumental movers, because *ex hypothesi* they will be moved movers, and nothing will be like a principal mover. And so nothing will be in motion.'[1] Thus stated, this argument, as Aquinas says, 'comes to the same as' the previous argument; and it contains the same equivocation. If the existence of instrumental movers is held to be proved by the principle 'whatever is in motion is moved by something else', then to move instrumentally must simply to be a moved mover; to be a principal mover will be, in the first premiss, to be an earlier mover, and in the second premiss, to be an unmoved mover. The argument of the *Physics* is not fairly represented by Aquinas; Aristotle starts from a distinction between movers who move by means of something else (e.g. a man pushing a stone with a lever) and movers who move by means of themselves (a man pushing a stone with his own body). On this account there would be no contradiction in the notion of a non-instrumental moved mover (e.g. a man pushing a stone with his body while being pushed by another). But to discuss Aristotle's difficult argument would take us too far from the First Way.

So much, then, for Aquinas' arguments against the infinite regress. We must return, in conclusion, to the principle that whatever is in motion is moved by something else. The objections made earlier to this principle were all drawn from everyday phenomena; no counterexample was used which might not have been observed in a medieval kitchen.

[1] Id quod movet instrumentaliter, non potest movere nisi sit aliquid quod principaliter moveat. Sed si in infinitum procedatur in moventibus et motis, omnia erunt quasi instrumentaliter moventia, quia ponentur sicut moventia mota, nihil autem erit sicut principale movens. Ergo nihil movebitur.

We must now ask how this principle, so fundamental in Aristotelean mechanics, has fared since the time of Newton. Newton's first law of motion states that every body perseveres in its state of rest, or of uniform motion in a right line, unless it is compelled to change that state by forces impressed thereon. Does not this law stand in direct opposition to the Aristotelean principle that whenever a body is in motion something distinct from it must be causing its motion?

It is true that Newton's law does not by itself account for the origin and presence of motion in the universe. Newton himself said: 'By this principle alone there never could be any motion in the world. Some other principle was necessary for putting bodies into motion; and now they are in motion, some other principle is necessary for conserving their motion' (General Scholium, quoted by Wallace). And Descartes, who anticipated Newton in enunciating the principle, said that the general cause of motion could be none other than God himself. 'He created matter along with motion and rest in the beginning; and now, merely by his ordinary cooperation, he preserves just the quantity of motion and rest in the material world that he put there in the beginning' (*Principles of Philosophy* II, 36).

None the less, it seems that Newton's law wrecks the argument of the First Way. For at any given time, the rectilinear uniform motion of a body can be explained by the principle of inertia in terms of the body's own previous motion without appeal to any other agent. And there seems no *a priori* reason why this explanatory process should not go backwards for ever. Newton's law will not explain how motion began; but how do we know that motion had a beginning? Aristotle himself, after all, thought motion was eternal. At the very least, on Newton's principles, there would be no more difficulty about motion *ab aeterno* than about the immobility *ab aeterno* of an unmoved mover. As Gilson has put it 'according to the law of inertia it is no more difficult to account for motion than to account for rest. That which is moving continues to move in virtue of the same property of matter by which it remains at rest unless acted on by some external force'. (Gilson (1), 61).

Faced with the Newtonian difficulties, Thomists have reacted in two principal ways. Some have simply abandoned the Aristotelean axiom in so far as it applies to local motion. Thus S. Vanni Rovighi says that the principle of inertia does not invalidate the First Way, but merely proves that local motion is not *motus* in the required sense (Vanni Rovighi, 345). R. Masi says that local motion is merely an extrinsic variation, not a real transition from potentiality to actuality in a body, since one position in space is no more perfect than another. He considers that the First Way would be better based on the principle 'whatever is accelerated is accelerated by something else' (Masi, 3ff). Presumably, so reconstructed, it would conclude to the existence of an unaccelerated accelerator.

The second reaction may be called the counter-attack with Mach. According to Newton, inertial motion took place in a straight line relative to absolute space. Berkeley, in his *De Motu*, critical of absolute motion and absolute space, maintained that inertial motion needed a reference frame, which was provided by the system of fixed stars. Mach took Berkeley's criticism a stage further. On his theory, the fixed stars provided not only the reference frame for the unaccelerated motions of bodies, but also the causal explanation of them: that is to say, the inertia of any body was determined by the masses of the universe and their distribution. The scholastic cosmologist P. Hoenen, having related the history of the concept of inertia from Aristotle to Mach, concluded 'inertial motion too demands an efficient cause, a real activity distinct from the body considered as in motion'. This efficient cause, he added, 'will not be a force in the technical sense in which this word is used in mechanics since force is there defined as the efficient cause of acceleration'. But, he thought, the scholastic adage 'whatever is in motion is moved by something else' remains valid; and he was himself inclined to identify the 'something else' in the case of inertial motion as waves in the aether. He thought it a

mistake for scholastics to exclude local motion from the First
Way. 'The classical argument from motion can still be up-
held' (Hoenen, 493–5 1).

Einstein, in the general theory of relativity, amalgamated
inertia and gravitation: the same quality of a body, he said,
manifests itself in different circumstances as inertia and as
weight. Instead of bodies having a tendency to travel in
straight lines through absolute space, we are to think of
particles guided along world-lines in a field determined by
the structure of space-time. Restated in terms of general
relativity, Mach's theory would amount to the claim that
the structure of space-time which provides the guiding field
is exhaustively determined by the large-scale distribution of
matter in the universe; so that if there were no matter there
would be no space-time metric. Einstein himself, when he
proposed the theory of general relativity, was convinced that
it was absolutely necessary to generalize Mach's principle
in this way; but subsequent experimental work has made it
a matter of dispute how far it is possible to do so.[1]

I am unqualified to have an opinion about this dispute.
But let us suppose that an explanation of inertia in full con-
formity with Mach's programme was forthcoming. How
would this affect the principle that whatever is in motion is
moved by something else? Aristotle would be vindicated to
this extent, that uniform local motion, and not only acceleration, would be shown to demand and receive a causal
explanation. But nothing resembling a reduction of inertia
to gravitation could salvage the use made of the principle
in the First Way. For the gravitational attraction of two
bodies is mutual, whereas the Aristotelean relation of
'moving' must be an asymmetrical one if it is to lead to an
unmoved mover. If A can move B while B moves A in the
same respect, the principle that whatever is in motion is
moved by something else can be verified in a universe in

---

[1] See Jammer, 190–196, on which the last paragraph is based. For
a recent attempt to implement Mach's programme, presented in a
popular fashion, see Sciama.

which there are no unmoved movers, but only two bodies, each in motion and each moving the other.

The effect of a successful implementation of Mach's principle would simply be to remove one counterexample to the Aristotelean principle, namely, that of bodies in uniform motion. There remain the pre-Newtonian counterexamples mentioned above, and in particular, the vital movements of living beings. However, these are *prima facie* counterexamples also to the law of inertia, so that Aristotle is no worse off than Newton in this respect. Any explanation which shows these cases to be merely apparent counterexamples to Newton's law will show them to be merely apparent counterexamples to Aristotle's axiom also.

If inertia were successfully explained solely in terms of the distribution of matter in the universe, two questions would remain which might be pressed by someone interested in proving the existence of God. First, he might ask for an explanation of the existence of the matter to be distributed. Consideration of the propriety of this question must be postponed until we discuss the Third Way. Secondly, he might ask for an explanation of the laws which in the new complete explanation supersede the Newtonian ones. To what extent is such a request reasonable?

It is clear that any explanation which consisted in deriving the new laws in their turn from other laws of wider generality and greater predictive power would leave the door open to another question of the same kind: why do *these* laws hold? There seem to be three possible positions one can take up about this whole question-and-answer process.

1. There is no theoretical end to the process, no end to the possibility of further explanation of this kind. At each point in the history of science we accept some explanations as basic, but these are later shown to be derivative, and there can be no such thing as an explanation which is, in the nature of things, basic.

2. There can be physical laws which are, in themselves and not just from a parochial viewpoint, basic. For Descartes, mechanistic explanations — explanations in terms of local

motion and the geometrical properties of matter — were basic in the sense that it was theoretically impossible to replace them with a more fundamental physical explanation, since geometrical extension was the essence of matter. On such a view the basic laws of physics are basic in virtue of exhibiting the special necessity believed to belong to the propositions of geometry. They thus need no causal explanation any more than truths of geometry do.

3. Descartes himself, it is well known, believed that even truths of geometry needed a causal explanation: they held because God freely made them to hold. On this view the ultimate explanation of why physical laws hold lies in the will of God. Clearly, this position could be held also by someone who did not think that physics was ultimately reducible to geometry. Such a view would give as the ultimate explanation of all laws something which was not itself a law-type explanation, so no regress is generated. Of course, there remains the question 'Why did God so will?', which asks for the Creator's reasons. Here again, several answers might seem possible. Perhaps God had no reason, one might say; one can explain a state of affairs as the result of an irrational action no less than as a result of a reasoned action. Or one might say that God had his reasons, but we cannot expect to know them; or that he had reasons which we might be able to guess at or even be told. There are difficulties about all these answers which we need not go into. The essential point to notice about any answer in terms of God's will is that it presupposes that explanations in terms of the choice of a voluntary agent are irreducible to explanations in terms of laws. This is something which, at the level of human agency, is a matter of debate; and it is a topic to which we shall return in discussing the Fifth Way.

I do not know which of these reactions is the correct one to the question 'Why do the ultimate physical laws hold?' The problem they concern is irrelevant to the First Way. For the First Way, true to its Aristotelean origins, does not raise the question why any laws of motion hold or why natural bodies have the natures and tendencies they do have.

The unmoved mover to which it argues is not the Author of Nature, but the efficient cause of the actual motions of substances in the world. And for the reasons we have seen, it does not succeed in showing that this efficient cause need be anything outside the world of matter. First, if it is to preserve from falsification the maxim on which it depends, it cannot insist that the relation of movement be asymmetrical; in which case there is no danger of an infinite regress, since a number of bodies within the world can cause each other's movement.[1] Secondly, even if there were an infinite regress of movers, it has not been shown that this leads to any absurdity.[2] Thirdly, the Aristotelean maxim has to be restricted to *per se* movement if it is to be defensible; but in that case an unmoved mover is a mover which is not *per se* moved; but any living being will count as an unmoved mover in these terms.[3] Fourthly, the argument at best shows that movement of any particular kind must originate in a being which is not moved in that particlar manner; it will not take us to a being which is unchanging in all respects, as it must if Aquinas is to be justified in saying of this being 'this all men think of as God'.[4] We may echo the words of the sixteenth-century Jesuit commentator Suarez. 'Taken by itself, this argument is shown in many ways impotent to prove there is anything immaterial in reality, let alone that there is a first and uncreated substance.'[5]

[1] See above, p. 14.　　[2] See above, p. 15.
[3] See above, p. 27.　　[4] See above, p. 23.
[5] Hoc autem medium per se ac praecise sumptum multis medis invenitur inefficax ad demonstrandum esse in rerum natura aliquam substantiam immaterialem, nedum ad demonstrandum primam et increatam substantiam. (*Disputationes metaphysicae* XXIX, 1, 7; quoted Owens (1), 35.)

3

The Second Way

The second way is based on the notion of efficient causation. In the observable world we discover an order of efficient causes, but no case is found, or ever could be found, of something efficiently causing itself. Such a thing would have to be prior to itself, which is impossible. Now it is impossible to go on for ever in a series of efficient causes. For in every ordered series of efficient causes the first member of the series causes the intermediate member or members, which in turn cause the final member. If you eliminate a cause you eliminate its effect, so there will not be final or intermediate members in the series unless there is a first member. But if the series goes on forever, then there will be no first efficient cause; and so there will be no final effect and no intermediate efficient cause, which is obviously false. Therefore it is necessary to posit some first efficient cause, to which everyone gives the name 'God'.[1]

---

[1] Secunda via est ex ratione causae efficientis. Invenimus enim in istis sensibilibus esse ordinem causarum efficientium; nec tamen invenitur nec est possibile quod aliquid sit causa efficiens sui ipsius, quia sic esset prius seipso quod est impossibile. Non autem est possibile quod in causis efficientibus procedatur in infinitum. Quia in omnibus causis efficientibus ordinatis primum est causa medii et medium est causa ultimi (sive media sint plura sive unum tantum), remota autem causa removetur effectus. Ergo si non fuerit primum in causis efficientibus non erit ultimum nec medium. Sed si procedatur in infinitum in causis efficientibus non erit prima causa efficiens, et sic non erit nec

Like the First Way, the Second Way presupposes an Aristotelean background. Aristotle, in his philosophical lexicon in *Metaphysics Delta*, distinguishes four types of causes, or perhaps rather four types of explanation. First, he says, there is that of which and from which a thing is made, such as the bronze of a statue and the silver of a cup. This is called the material cause. Second, he says, there is the form and pattern of a thing: this is what is expressed by the definition, which tells us what it is to be a thing of that kind. Aquinas, in his commentary, gives as an example the definition 'two legged land animal'. Plato's Ideas or Forms, as he points out, were supposed to be patterns causing or explaining things in this fashion: and this type of cause, accordingly, is named 'formal cause'. The third type of cause mentioned by Aristotle is the origin of a change or state of rest in a thing: he gives as examples a person giving advice, a father who begets a child, 'and in general any maker in relation to what it makes, and any changer in relation to what it changes'. The fourth and last type of cause is the end or goal, that for the sake of which something is done; it is the type of explanation we give if someone asks us why we are walking and we reply 'for the sake of our health'. This is explanation by final causes.[1]

Aquinas took over the doctrine of the four causes; it is the third type which he has in mind when he speaks of efficient causes, as in the Second Way. In his commentary on Aristotle's metaphysics, he calls this third kind of cause 'moving or efficient cause', and throughout his work he uses '*causa movens*' and '*causa efficiens*' more or less as synonyms with each other and with '*causa agens*'.[2] It follows that the causal phenomena and relationships which form the basic premise of the Second Way overlap with those considered in the First Way; for wherever a body A is moved by a body B, B

---

effectus ultimus nec causae efficientes mediae, quod patet esse falsum. Ergo necesse est ponere aliquam causam efficientem primam, quam omnes Deum nominant.

[1] Aristotle, *Metaphysics*, Δ, 1013a 24 ff. *In Met* V, 765.

[2] See Preller, 68.

stands in the relation of efficient cause to A. However, the First Way looks at such phenomena from the point of view of the effect or body acted upon, while the Second Way considers the process from the other end, starting from the agent rather than from the patient, from the movers rather than the things in motion. Moreover the Second Way includes within its purview agents which are not really 'movers' in the sense of the first way. The father of a child is not a mover of the child, since he does not change the child, but rather brings him into existence. Here, therefore, we have a *causa efficiens* without a *res mota*. But though the father does not cause a change in the child, he does cause a change in the world, since he begets the child by giving a new form to pre-existent material. For Aristotle, who believed in an ever-lasting material universe, all efficient causality would be re-describable in this way as the initiation of a change in pre-existent material, and so as a movement. But for Aquinas, who believed that God created the universe out of nothing, there was at least one efficient cause that could act without being *eo ipso* a mover. So he has a special interest in occasionally separating out the two notions.

It may be for this reason that Aquinas has two distinct Ways corresponding to two different aspects of Aristotle's efficient causality. If we take these two Ways together we find that the distinction between the Five Ways reflects the distinction between the Four Causes. This is most obvious in the case of the Fifth Way, which clearly depends on the notion of final causality; but the Third Way, as we shall see, concerns itself initially with material causality, and the Fourth argues from formal causality. The Five Ways have a formal structure in common which is applied in turn to the Four Causes, and the different types of causality provide different contents for this formal structure. If the identity of the structure is not immediately apparent, this is because in the different arguments different premises are left implicit and different additional conclusions are argued for. Basically, each of the Five Ways takes a two-place relational predicate 'R' and shows the relation in question to be irreflexive (nothing has R to itself) and transitive (if a stands in the relation R to b, and b to c, then a also has R to c). It concludes from this that either there is an endless series of things standing in the relation R to each other, or else there is something to which others may have R which does not itself stand in the relation R to anything. In the First Way, 'aRb' is to be interpreted as 'a is being moved by b'; in the Second as 'a is efficiently caused by b'; in the Third as 'a can cease to exist by turning into b'; in the Fourth as 'a is less noble, true, good than b'; in the Fifth as 'a is directed to a goal by b, who is higher in the scale of cognitive powers'. These predicates recognizably correspond to the Four Causes: their correspondence to the Five Ways will become clear, it is to be hoped, in the course of the book.[1]

This basic formal structure is a sound one.[2] For the following formula is not satisfiable in a finite domain:

$$\forall x - Rxx \ \& \ \forall x \, \forall y \, \forall z \, (Rxy \ \& \ Ryz \ \to \ Rxz) \ \& \ \forall x \exists y Rxy$$

For a given interpretation of 'R', this formula says in effect that the relation R is irreflexive and transitive, and that everything stands in the relation R to something or other. If, therefore, we have a relation which we know to be irreflexive and transitive, and we know that the domain of the relation is finite, we can conclude that not everything stands in that relation to something. In symbols: we conclude

$$- \forall x \exists y Rxy$$

and from that $\exists x - \exists y Rxy$
which, if we interpret 'R' as '... is caused by', says

There is an uncaused thing.

In his book *The Foundations of Mathematics*, E. W. Beth has drawn attention to a formula which he calls 'The

---

[1] The most apparently forced of these assimilations is the third. It should be said at once that this interpretation corresponds better to the version in ScG 1, 15 than to that in the *Summa Theologiae*.

[2] On the formal structure of the First Way, see Salamucha and Clark.

Principle of the Absolute'.[1] This states that if there are
entities x and y which stand to each other in the relation R,
then there is an entity z with the following property: for
any entity w which is distinct from z, we have (i) w has the
relation R to z, and (ii) z does not have the relation R to w.
He symbolizes the principle as follows:

$$\exists x \exists y Rxy \;\rightarrow\; \exists z \forall w (w \neq z \rightarrow [Rwz \;\&\; -Rzw])$$

Beth remarks that Aristotle made frequent use of the
principle, and adds that belief in it 'is the basis for several
of the traditional proofs for the existence of God'. But the
principle, he points out, is not a logical truth, as can be
shown by giving counterexamples. Let 'Rxy' be interpreted
'x is a segment of a line which is larger than the segment y
of the same line'. Then it follows from the Principle of the
Absolute that there must be a segment w which is smaller
than any other segment. But there cannot be any such
segment, as Aristotle showed himself aware in his discussion
of Zeno's paradoxes. Hence, Beth concludes, the principle
cannot be a logical truth.

The conclusion is, of course, true; and Beth could have
found a counterexample involving a merely finite domain
(e.g. '... is the spouse of...'). But I think Beth was mistaken
if he thought that his principle was at the basis of proofs
such as the Five Ways. The 'principle of the absolute' used
by Aquinas (and also by Aristotle in the instances actually
quoted by Beth) depends on the relation in question being
transitive and irreflexive; so that the formulation of the
principle should include in its antecedent the conditions for
irreflexivity and transitivity. It would then read

$$\exists x \; \exists y Rxy \;\&\; \forall x - Rxx \;\&\; \forall x \forall y \forall z (Rxy \;\&\; Ryz \rightarrow Rxz) \;\rightarrow$$
$$\exists z \; \forall w (w \neq z \rightarrow [Rwz \;\&\; -Rzw)]$$

This principle, too, is not difficult to falsify in a finite
domain: the interpretation '... is a descendant of ...' will
falsify it in the domain of human beings, unless we are all

---

[1] Beth, 9. I am indebted for this reference to Mr. W. Harris.

indeed descended from a single pair and Eve counts as a descendant of Adam. However, if the conclusion is weakened so that it states that the absolute entity does not itself stand in the relation R, but says nothing about others standing in that relation to it, we get

$$\exists x \exists y Rxy \ \& \ \forall x - Rxx \ \& \ \forall x \ \forall y \ \forall z \ (Rxy \ \& \ Ryz \ \to \ Rxz) \ \to$$
$$\to \exists z \ \forall w - Rzw$$

and this indeed is valid for every finite domain.[1]

It is unwise, therefore, for a critic of the Five Ways to attack their formal structure. To refute one of them one must rather show either that the relation in question does not hold of anything, or that it does not have the properties of transitivity and irreflexivity, or that there is no reason to restrict it to a finite domain. Alternatively, one may show that something which did not bear that relation to anything would not necessarily be a candidate for being called 'God'. In fact it may also be the case — as we have already seen *a propos* of the First Way — that the verb used by Aquinas for the relation bears several senses; and that in one sense it will stand for a relation with the appropriate formal properties, but not one which would serve in a definition of God; and in another sense it will be apt to mark a property of God but cannot be shown to hold between entities in the observable universe.

With this in mind, we must examine the relation of efficient causation. Of all Aristotle's types of causes, this is the one which comes nearest to the modern sense of 'cause'; but there are still important differences between the two notions. Since the time of Hume, it is natural to think of a cause as an event of some sort. Events of kind A lead to events of kind B, and this is something we discover inductively. This is not the notion of cause with which Aquinas operates. For him, efficient causes are substantial agents. We must recall that the paradigm cases of causation for an

---

[1] Since R is irreflexive, we have $\forall w \ \forall z \ (w = z \to - Rzw)$ and so the antecedent of the consequent may be dropped.

Aristotelean are heating and wetting. If A heats B, then A produces heat in B, B receives heat from A, A changes B; and in general, if ϕ takes the place of any such verb, when A ϕs B, A produces ϕness in B, B receives ϕness from A, and A changes B. Now *prima facie*, all these relations between A and B are transitive and asymmetrical; for instance if A is heating B and B is heating C, then A is heating C; and on the other hand if A is heating B, then B is not heating A. But if the relations are asymmetrical, they are also irreflexive; for nothing can stand in an asymmetrical relation to itself. For it follows from what we have just said that if A is heating A then A is not heating A; and so there cannot be a case of A heating A.

Two of the best known Aristotelean theses about causation were that effects were like their causes and that causes were prior to their effects. The first thesis is readily intelligible in the light of the preceding discussion: the likeness between cause and effect is precisely in the ϕness which B receives from A which must itself already possess ϕness (e.g. only what is hot heats). The priority of cause over effect need not be temporal — to quote the popular medieval counterinstance, an everlasting foot might cause an everlasting footprint in everlasting sand — but a cause A must be prior to an effect B in the sense that you can have an A without a B but not a B without an A. (Priority in the number series, Aristotle thought, was a particular case of this: 2 comes before 3 because you can have 2 men without 3 men but not 3 men without 2 men.)[1]

In discussing the First Way in the previous chapter we saw reason to doubt whether the relation of *moving* is both transitive and irreflexive as it seems at first sight. It appeared that it had not been shown that there was anything incoherent in the idea of something's moving itself. However, the cases which are covered by the Second Way and not by the First are those in which something is brought into existence; and there seems to be a special incoherence in the

[1] E. E. 1218a 6.

notion of something's bringing itself into existence. The generation of one member of a species by another seems to provide an irreproachable example of an irreflexive causal relation. Man begets man: the son is a man like the father, and the father is prior to the son. In human generation, if anywhere, we have a relation of efficient causality which will provide a premise for the Second Way.

It is no part of Aquinas' premise that every event has a cause. Indeed, this causal principle is something which he expressly denied. Fortuitous events, chance coincidences, as such have no causes. If a man is killed by a falling meteorite, there will be a cause for the fall of the meteorite, and perhaps a reason for the man's presence in the fatal spot; but there will be no cause for the man's being killed by the meteorite (Ia, 115, 6). Aquinas did indeed believe in the principle later questioned by Hume, that every beginning of real existence has a cause. But he did not believe in this as a particular case of a universal determinism.

If a parent is an efficient cause of a child, then there can be no doubt that there are at least some efficient causes in the world. But what does Aquinas mean when he tells us that there is an *order* of efficient causes? From the context one might think that he had in mind the series of ancestors of a particular man; father, grandfather, greatgrandfather and so on. But this is not so, as we see from Ia, 46, 2 and 7, where Aquinas makes clear that he sees nothing incoherent in the idea that this series might go back for ever. Such a series would merely be a series of efficient causes *per accidens*, he explains. 'It is not impossible to go on for ever *per accidens* in a series of efficient causes . . . as a smith may act by using many different hammers, *per accidens*, if one after the other is broken. For it is not essential for any particular hammer to act after the action of another, and it is likewise not essential for any particular man, *qua* begetter, to be begotten by another man; for he begets *qua* man, and not *qua* son of another man . . . Hence it is not impossible to go on for ever in the series of men begetting men; but such a thing would be impossible if the generation of one man depended

on another and on an element, and on the sun, and so on to
infinity'.[1]

It is this second series: man — element — sun which is the
series of efficient causes *per se*. As Aquinas says, following
Aristotle (*Phys.* 2, 194b 4) 'man and the sun beget man'.
The series of causes in the Second Way, like the series of
movers in the First, does not stretch backwards in time, but
stretches into the heavens simultaneously. It is this series
which must come to an end with God.

What is meant by saying that man is generated by man
'and the sun'? Fr. H. McCabe, O.P., explains thus. 'It is
not an adequate explanation of the coming to be of a man
that there should be another man — if it is puzzling that there
should be one man, it is no less puzzling that there should
be two — there is required a cause of higher order to account
for the fact that there are men at all, a cause that there is
such a species. Perhaps in modern terms we might substitute the whole order of nature, the course of evolution,
and so on, for the sun, but it is in any case clear that it is one
thing to ask how it happens that there is a particular species
in the world and another to ask about the coming to be of a
particular member of it.'[2] McCabe's point is correct, but is
doubly irrelevant to the Second Way. In the first place, the
Second Way is seeking to explain not the coming to be of a
son, but the act of begetting of a father. In the second place,
the course of evolution is something in the past, whereas the
higher-order cause which Aquinas means by 'the sun' is a
contemporary cause. This is recognized by P. Garrigou-

---

[1] Per accidens in infinitum procedere in causis agentibus non
reputatur impossibile . . . sicut artifex agit multis martellis per accidens,
quia unus post unum frangitur. Accidit ergo huic martello, quod agat
post actionem alterius martelli. Et similiter accidit huic homini,
inquantum generat, quod sit generatus ab alio: generat enim inquantum homo, et non inquantum est filius alterius hominis . . . Unde
non est impossibile quod homo generatur ab homine in infinitum.
Esset autem impossibile, si generatio huius hominis dependeret ab hoc
homine, et a corpore elementari, et a sole, et sic in infinitum.

[2] McCabe, 103.

Lagrange, who explains the puzzling passage by saying that without earth, water, air and heat generation would be impossible. 'Science still agrees that the generation of a child depends upon the father and upon the heat necessary for the conservation of life on the earth. This is the empirical basis of the argument.'[1] But this is to make the series of simultaneous causes simply a series of necessary conditions; and then it is hard to see why Aquinas should think the series cannot be an endless one, since the series of ancestors too is a series of necessary conditions (had my grandfathers not existed, nor should I) and he will allow this to be infinite.

In fact, Aquinas believed that the sun was very much more than a necessary condition of human generation. The human father, he explains in Ia 115, 3, in generation is a tool of the sun. The active qualities of the elements, such as heat and cold, are insufficient to explain the rise of substantial forms; so their causation must be attributed, following Aristotle, to a mobile active principle 'which by its presence and absence causes the phases of generation and corruption of bodies here on earth.' Such are the heavenly bodies. 'And so whatever begets here below, reproduces its kind as an instrument of a heavenly body.'[2]

For merely animal generation, the activity of the sun is more like a sufficient condition than a necessary condition. It is only where human freedom intervenes that it is impossible to predict the future from a study of the heavenly bodies. Because there is no bodily organ of intellect and will, human behaviour is not completely predictable from the stars. However, Aquinas tells us, since most men do not resist their bodily passions, astrologers are able to foretell

[1] Garrigou-Lagrange, 28.

[2] Necesse est ponere aliquod principium activum mobile, quod per sui praesentiam et absentiam causat varietatem circa generationem et corruptionem inferiorum corporum. Et huiusmodi sunt corpora caelestia. Et ideo quidquid in istis inferioribus generat, movet ad speciem sicut instrumentum caelestis corporis; secundum quod dicitur in II Physic, quod homo generat hominem et sol.

statistically the outcomes of wars and similar events. This is why their predictions, by and large, come true.[1]

It is by now clear that the series of causes from which the Second Way starts is a series whose existence is vouched for only by medieval astrology. The Second Way, like the First, starts from a series of simultaneous agents and not from a series stretching backwards in time; the Second Way, like the First, uses an equivocation between 'first = earlier' and 'first = unpreceded' to show that this series cannot be an infinite one.[2] But the First Way starts from an indisputable fact about the world; the Second starts from an archaic fiction.

There are, of course, genuine questions raised by the phenomenon of animal reproduction. Some of these have been given an answer by the patient empirical investigations of physiologists and biochemists since the middle ages: discoveries about spermatozoa, ova, genes and DNA make us incomparably better informed about the mechanism or generation than Aquinas was. But this information is irrelevant to the Second Way, since it falls within the realm not of efficient, but of formal, causality.

There are also, as McCabe points out, genuine questions about the origin of the species whose reproduction provides the basis of the Second Way. The theory of natural selection offers us efficient causes for this origin: the red teeth and red claws of organisms competing for survival. Perhaps these agents in their turn can be traced back in a causal chain to the hot and the cold and the wet and the dry acting upon some primeval soup, or whatever equivalents to these elements figure in contemporary cosmologies. But this

---

[1] Plures homines sequuntur passiones, quae sunt motus sensitivi appetitus, ad quas cooperari possunt corpora caelestia; pauci atuem sunt sapientes, qui huiusmodi passionibus resistant. Et ideo astrologi ut in pluribus vera possunt praedicere, et maxime in communi. Non autem in speciali: quia nihil prohibet aliquem hominem per liberum arbitrium passionibus resistere. Ia, 115, 4.

[2] See above, p. 26.

history too is irrelevant to the Second Way, which seeks a series of simultaneously active efficient causes.

The only convincing examples of such series given by Aquinas are human instruments: the levers, knives and axes used by masons, tailors and woodcutters (e.g. *De Pot* III, 7). Here indeed we have causes whose causing is caused by a simultaneously acting further cause. But such series cease with the human agent who is using the tool. There is no reason, outside archaic astronomy, to believe that a man, in begetting, is a member of such a series. If he is not, then of course we do have in a sense an uncaused cause; but the uncaused cause is the human parent and not any creator of the world.

4

The Third Way

The Third way is drawn from the possible and the necessary, and runs as follows. Some things we encounter have the possibility of being and of not being, since we find them being generated and corrupted, and accordingly with the possibility of being and not being. Now it is impossible for all that there is to be like that; because what has the possibility of not being, at some time is not. If therefore everything has the possibility of not being, at one time there was nothing. But if this were the case, there would be nothing even now, because what is not does not begin to be except through something which is; so if nothing was in being, it was impossible for anything to begin to be, and so there would still be nothing, which is obviously false. Not everything therefore has the possibility [of being and not being], but there must be something which is necessary. Now everything which is necessary either has the cause of its necessity outside itself, or it does not. Now it is not possible to go on for ever in a series of necessary beings which have a cause of their necessity, just as was shown in the case of efficient causes. So it is necessary to assume something which is necessary of itself, and has no cause of its necessity outside itself, but is rather the cause of necessity in other things, and this all men call God.[1]

*   *   *

[1] Tertia via est sumpta ex possibili et necessario, quae talis est. Invenimus enim in rebus quaedam quae sunt possibilia esse et non

In modern philosophy, it is often said that God is a necessary being, and that everything else is contingent. One of Leibniz's proofs for the existence of God concludes that there exists 'a necessary being, in whom essence involves existence, or in whom it suffices to be possible in order to be actual. Thus God alone (or the necessary Being) has this prerogative, that he must necessarily exist if he be possible.' If God is a necessary being in this sense, then 'there is a God' is a logically necessary proposition.

Before Aquinas, Avicenna operated with a concept of necessity similar to that of Leibniz. 'A necessary being is a being such that the supposition of its non-existence entails a contradiction. A possible being is a being such that no inconsistency arises whether it is supposed to exist or not.'[1] In his early writings, St. Thomas utilized this notion of necessity, according to which only God is a necessary being, and all creatures are contingent, since only in God does essence entail existence (*De Veritate* 10, 12c).

This is not the sense of necessity used in the Third Way. For Aquinas does not consider his proof of the existence of

---

esse, cum quaedam inveniantur generari et corrumpi et per consequens possibilia esse et non esse. Impossibile est autem omnia quae sunt, talia esse, quia quod possibile est non esse quandoque non est. Si igitur omnia sunt possibilia non esse aliquando nihil fuit in rebus. Sed si hoc est verum etiam nunc nihil esset, quia quod non est non incipit esse nisi per aliquid quod est. Si igitur nihil fuit ens, impossibile fuit quod aliquid inciperet esse, et sic modo nihil esset, quod patet esse falsum. Non ergo omnia entia sunt possibilia sed oportet aliquid esse necessarium in rebus. Omne autem necessarium vel habet causam suae necessitatis aliunde vel non habet. Non est autem possibile quod procedatur in infinitum in necessariis quae habent causam suae necessitatis, sicut nec in causis efficientibus, ut probatum est. Ergo necesse est ponere aliquid quod est per se necessarium non habens causam suae necessitatis aliunde, sed quod est causa necessitatis aliis, quod omnes dicunt Deum.

[1] Necesse-esse est ens quod si ponatur non esse implicat contradictionem. Possibile vero esse est illud quod sive ponatur esse sive non esse, non inde oritur repugnantia. (*Metaphysices compendium*, cited Jalbert, 21.)

God concluded when he has established that there exists a necessary being. On the contrary, he at once goes on to consider 'necessary beings who have the cause of their necessity outside themselves' a description which could not apply to God.

Guy Jalbert has shown that at the time of writing the *contra Gentiles* Aquinas was converted by the reading of Averroes to a doctrine of necessity different from that of Avicenna. Henceforth he defined necessity not in terms of essence and existence, but in terms of unalterability, following Aristotle's definition of the necessary as that which cannot be otherwise (*Metaphysics*Δ 1015a 34). In this sense something is necessarily the case if it cannot cease to be the case, and a being has necessary existence if it cannot cease to exist (ScG II, 30). Since Aquinas believed that the heavenly bodies, the human soul, and the angels were all naturally incapable of ceasing to exist, he was henceforth prepared to say that their existence was necessary and to call them necessary beings (Bodies: 1a, 105, 6, 1st objn; soul: 1a 75, 6, ad 2m; angels, 1a 50, 5 ad 3m). Not only God, then, but many creatures are necessary beings in Aquinas' mature system (Ia 44, 1, 2, and ad 2). (See Jalbert; Geach (2), 115, Kenny, (1).)

The Third Way, then, is not simply an argument from contingent being to necessary being. It does indeed start from contingent beings (things which 'have the possibility of being and of not being'), but it works through the existence of caused necessary beings, to the existence of a being whose necessity is uncaused, which alone, among necessary beings, can be called God.[1]

The first premise of the argument asserts the existence of

[1] Some scholastics distinguish between metaphysical contingency (essence not involving existence) and physical contingency (corruptibility). Using this distinction, we may say that the Third Way starts from beings which are both physically and metaphysically contingent and argues through beings which are physically necessary but metaphysically contingent to a being which is both physically and metaphysically necessary (Pattin).

things which have the possibility of being and not being (*possibilia esse et non esse*). This is asserted as a fact of experience: in the formulation of a parallel proof in the *contra Gentiles* (I, 15) we read: 'we see in the world some things which have the possibility of being and not being'.[1] We know what they have this possibility because they are 'generated and corrupted'.

It is clear enough in general what sort of thing Aquinas has in mind. Houses are built and destroyed, ice turns into water and into steam, shrubs spring up and wither away, animals and men are begotten and die. But it is not clear exactly what entities are being said to have the possibility of being and not being, nor exactly what is meant by this possibility.

First, is it individuals (like Socrates) or kinds (like mankind) which are said to have this possibility? Does the argument start from premises like 'Socrates is mortal' or from premises like 'man is mortal'? Secondly, is the class of things which have the possibility of being and not being co-extensive with the class of things which are generated and corrupted?[2] Thirdly, what kind of possibility is involved? Is it logical possibility, or something more? Fourthly, how should we take the tenses of the verbs in the phrase 'things which have the possibility of being and not being'? Do the things *now* have this possibility or is it just that at some time of their history they had, have, or will have the possibility? And is the 'being and not being' something to be done in the past, present, or future?

Let us start by trying to answer the last question, whose sense is probably the least clear. Take some individual now existing, such as Lyndon B. Johnson. He exists now, but

[1] Videmus in mundo quaedum quae sunt possibilia esse et non esse, scilicet generabilia et corruptibilia.

[2] In the *Summa Theologiae*, generation and corruption are said to entail the possibility of being and not being; in the *Summa contra Gentiles* 'things which have the possibility of being and not being' is followed by the gloss 'namely, things which can be generated and corrupted'.

there was a time when he did not exist. Now it is one of the most assured principles of modal logic, that whatever is the case, can be the case: *ab esse ad posse valet consequentia*, as medieval modal logicians said. (Prior, (1), 188). It therefore is now possible both for Johnson to exist and for him to have not existed in the remote past. This is one thing which we might mean by saying that Johnson 'has the possibility of being and not being'. And however long Johnson has lived or will live, throughout his history he has had, and will have, this possibility. But of course it is not the case that 'Johnson has the possibility of being and not being' has always been true; for before he existed there was no Johnson to have the possibility. Note that on this account something which always exists will always have the possibility of being, but not necessarily the possibility of not being; and consequently something which is a necessary being will be, *a fortiori*, a possible being.[1]

Lyndon Johnson, presumably, is not immortal; and so he has the possibility of not being in a sense stronger than that outlined in the last paragraph. After he dies, there will again be a time when he does not exist; consequently, we might say, he has the possibility of not being *in the future* as well as in the past. If, however, he were immortal, and could never cease to exist, he would still have the possibility of being and not being in the weaker sense, but not in the stronger sense. Now which sense has the expression in the Third Way? It must be remembered that Aquinas, unlike Aristotle, believed in the doctrine of creation. For Aristotle, the world had always existed and would always exist; consequently the heavenly bodies did not have in either sense the possibility of not being. So they could be called necessary beings in the fullest sense (*Metaphysics* H 1050b 13–20). But for Aquinas, the world had been created once upon a time and human souls were created from time to time as human bodies were developed for them; consequently, the

---

[1] This is worth remarking since some authors treat '*possbile esse et non esse*' and '*possibile esse*' as synonyms. See Finili, 31.

heavenly bodies and human souls had the possibility of being and not being in the past but not in the future. None the less, as we have seen, Aquinas is prepared to call them necessary beings; consequently, the possibility of being and not being, which in the Third Way is contrasted with the necessity which may belong to such imperishable creatures, must be the possibility of *ceasing to be*, the possibility of not being in the future.

But Aquinas believed that God was omnipotent, and could do whatever did not involve a contradiction (1a, 25, 3). Even if heavenly bodies and human souls are naturally everlasting, then, it must be possible for God to destroy them by annihilation. Does it not follow, then, that all creatures have, in the strong sense, the possibility of being and not being? Aquinas considered this question in the *contra Gentiles*. 'There are among created things some whose existence is necessary without any qualification or condition. For the existence of any being is necessary, without any qualification or condition, if that being has no possibility of not existing. Now some things have been brought into being by God in such a way that in their nature there is a power of not existing. That is because the matter in them is in potency to another form. Those things, therefore, in which there is no matter, or if there is, in which the matter is not in potentiality to another form, have no power of not existing . . . It may be said that things which come from nothing have a tendency, so far as in them lies, to return to nothing; and that therefore all creatures have a power of not existing. But this is manifestly a bad argument. It is said that created things return to nothing in the same way as they come from nothing. But to say that they come from nothing is simply to refer to the power of the creator. There is not therefore in these creatures a power of not existing; but there is a power in the creator of choosing either to give them existence or to cease keeping them in existence.'[1]

---

[1] Sunt enim quaedam in rebus creatis quae simpliciter et absolute necesse est esse. Illas enim res simpliciter et absolute necesse est esse

This passage makes clear that the 'possibility' which
Aquinas is talking about is not merely logical possibility.
He did recognize such a type of possibility, and discussed
it elsewhere in the same book: 'we call propositions possible
but not necessary', he says, 'when there is no necessary connection between the subject and the predicate . . . When
something is said to be possible in this sense no reference is
made to any power, but simply that it is neither necessary
nor impossible, as Aristotle says in *Metaphysics* V; just as
"this triangle has two sides equal" is a possible proposition;
but this has no reference to any power, since in mathematics
there is neither power nor change.'[1] Aquinas can agree that
in the sense in which 'this triangle has two sides equal' is a
possible proposition, so also is 'the sun has ceased to exist'.
But the logical possibility of the sun's ceasing to exist does
not mean that the sun has a power of not existing; and the
passage quoted in the previous paragraph makes it clear that
this is what is in question. In the Third Way — and thus we
answer our third question — in saying that some things have
the possibility of not being, Aquinas does not mean that

---

in quibus non est possibilitas ad non esse. Quaedam autem res sic sunt
a Deo in esse productae ut in earum natura sit potentia ad non esse.
Quod quidem contingit ex hoc quod materia in eis est in potentia ad
aliam forman. Illae igitur res in quibus vel non est materia, vel, si est,
non est possibilis ad aliam formam, non habent potentiam ad non
esse . . . Si autem dicatur quod ea quae sunt ex nihilo, quantum est de
se, in nihilum tendunt; et sic omnibus creaturis inest potentia ad non
esse: —manifestum est hoc non sequi. Dicuntur enim res creatae eo
modo in nihilum tendere quo sunt ex nihilo. Quod quidem non est nisi
secundum potentiam agentis. Sic igitur et rebus creatis non inest
potentia ad non esse: sed Creatori inest potentia ut eis det esse vel eis
desinat esse influere (ScG II, 30).

[1] Possibilia enuntiabilia dicimus quando non est necessarius ordo
praedicati ad subiectum . . . illo modo quo non dicitur aliquid possible
secundum aliquam potentiam, sed quod non necesse est esse nec
impossibile est esse, ut Philosophus tradit in V. Metaph: sicut triangu-
lum habere duo latera aequalia est enuntiabile possible, non tamen
secundum aliquam potentiam, cum in mathematicis non sit potentia
neque motus.

there are some things whose non-existence involves no contradiction, but that there are some things which have a power of not existing.

Difficulties at once arise. What is such a power, and how does Aquinas know that there are things which have it? For once we leave aside logical possibility, we leave aside the principle *ab esse ad posse valet consequentia*: the fact that a thing ceases to exist does not show that it has a power of not existing. The answer to this objection is given in the first passage quoted above: things have a power of not existing if 'the matter in them is in potency to another form', i.e. if the stuff they consist of is such that they can turn into something else. Earth, air, fire, and water, Aquinas believed, consisted of mutable stuff of this kind and could turn into each other; not so the sun and moon and stars, made out of an immutable quintessence, or fifth kind of stuff. Human souls and angelic spirits, on the other hand, are not made out of any stuff at all, *a fortiori* not out of stuff capable of assuming different forms. And so he says 'Those things in which there is no matter, or if there is, in which the matter is not in potency to another form, have no power of not existing.'

That is why—and here is the answer to our second question—Aquinas appeals to the fact of generation and corruption to show the possibility of being and not being in creatures. The words *'generari'* and *'corrumpi'* and their Greek equivalents are sometimes translated 'coming to be and passing away'; but not every kind of coming to be is a case of generation. If something is instantaneously created it comes into existence; but it is not generated, in Aquinas' sense, unless it comes into existence from pre-existent matter. Similarly, annihilation is not corruption; the paradigm of corruption, as the word suggests, is when an animal dies and turns into dust. Generation need not be, as the word suggests, the production of one living being by another—there can be artificial generation, like the building of a house (*In Met*, VII, 1404);—but it is always a coming into existence from something else, as a house is made out of bricks and wood (*In Met* VII, 1416).

There remains a difficulty when Aquinas says in ScG 1, 15 that we see *generabilia*. We do see corruptible human beings; but before they are begotten, they are not there to be generable, still less to be visible. This was what promoted the first question above: are the generables and corruptibles kinds or individuals? By now we can give the answer fairly simply. What we see are individuals which have the power of turning into something other than they are now: Fs, say, which may turn into Gs. We know they have this power because they belong to kinds, other members of which have actually turned into something other than they were: other Fs did become Gs. These Fs we see can, if you like, be regarded as generable Gs; but as there are problems about the individuation of the not yet existent Gs, this is a dangerous form of speech. And Aquinas himself, in the commentary on the *De Caelo* praises Aristotle for using the phrase 'generated and corruptible things' in a similar context, rather than 'generable and corruptible things' or 'generated and corrupted things'. 'He says "generated",' wrote Aquinas, 'using the factual term, and "corruptible", using the modal term, because since generation goes from non-being to being, and corruption from being to non-being, what is generable is not yet in existence, but only what is generated; and only what is corruptible is in existence, not what is already corrupted.'[1]

Interpreted in this manner, the Third Way starts from an indubitably true premise. The interchange of matter between bodies and their environment is considerably more complicated than Aristotle or Aquinas realized; but the progress of chemistry and biology has confirmed rather than refuted the premise that there exist generable and corruptible beings, i.e. bodies which consist of matter which

---

[1] Ideo autem posuit genitum secundum actum, et corruptible secundum potentiam, quia cum generatio sit de non esse in esse, corruptio de esse in non esse, illud quod est generabile nondum est ens, sed solum id quod iam est genitum: e converso autem id quod est corruptibile est ens, non autem id quod iam est corruptum (*In de Caelo et Mundo*, I, 24, 8). Cited by Gonzalez Pola.

has existed in other forms and which can survive in altered form their own destruction.

The next sentence in the Third Way raises a textual problem. The text of the Leonine edition reads: '*impossible est autem omnia quae sunt talia semper esse*', which is most plausibly translated: 'it is impossible for all things of this kind always to exist'. This translation is, like the Latin, ambiguous between 'it is impossible that anything of this kind should always exist' (i.e. nothing of this kind can exist for ever) and 'it is impossible that everything of this kind should always exist' (i.e. not everything of this kind can exist for ever). The latter version is the most natural reading of the Latin, the former the interpretation which best fits the context. Other manuscripts, which many commentators prefer, read '*impossible est autem omnia quae sunt talia esse*'; 'it is impossible for all that there is to be like this'. This reading makes the argument read much more smoothly; but in substance is not very different from the first way of interpreting the alternative reading. Either way the argument starts with the premise 'whatever has the possibility of not being at some time or other is not' and concludes 'not everything has the possibility of not being'. The steps common to both versions of the argument may be set out thus.[1]

(1)   Whatever has the possibility of not being, at some time or other is not.

(2)   If everything has the possibility of not being, then at some time or other nothing is.

(3)   If at some time or other nothing is, then there is nothing now.

(4)   It is not the case that there is nothing now.

(5)   Not everything has the possibility of not being.

---

[1] Using 'Qx' for 'x has the possibility of not being', 'Ext' for 'x exists at t', 'n' for 'now', 'Mp' for 'it is possible that p', and quantifying over times, we may symbolize as follows.

(1) $\forall x(Qx \rightarrow \exists t - Ext)$

(2) $\forall x \ Qx \rightarrow \exists t \ \forall x - Ext$

(3) $\exists t \forall x - Ext \rightarrow \forall x - Exn$

(4) $-\forall x - Exn$

(5) $-\forall x Qx$

(1a) $\forall x(Qx \rightarrow -M(\forall t Ezt))$

If the Leonine reading be accepted, then after step (1) there is intercalated a step (1*a*) as follows:

> (1*a*)   Whatever has the possibility of not being cannot exist at all times.

This step is presented as following from (1). It is hard to see how it does so, since from the fact that something does not exist for ever, it does not follow that it cannot exist for ever: we seem to have a violation of the principle *a non esse ad non posse non valet consequentia*. But in Aquinas' argument from (2) to (3) no appeal seems to be made to (1*a*) rather than to (1). Since the Leonine reading involves the introduction of an extra step which is both fallacious and useless, I have adopted the other reading, on which (5) is simply stated at the beginning of the argument as the conclusion to be proved.

Even with this reading, we seem to be faced with fallacies enough. First of all, premise (1) itself seems doubtful: why cannot there be something which has the power not to exist, but as a matter of fact always does exist? Secondly, (2) does not seem to follow from (1). To be sure, from (1) and 'everything has the possibility of not being' we can get

> (6) Each thing at some time or other is not.[1]

but this is not equivalent to, and does not entail

> (7) At some time or other, everything is not.[2]

To pass from (6) to (7) is to commit a fallacy known to logicians as the quantifier-shift fallacy. Its fallaciousness may be brought out by the parallel argument that since every road leads somewhere, there is somewhere (e.g. Rome) to which every road leads.

Consider now the principle 'what has the possibility of not being, at some time is not'. One expression which has excited commentators in this principle is 'at some time' ('*quandoque*'). Some commentators have spoken of a 'non-temporal' 'sometime'; by which they appear to mean that

---

[1] $\forall x \exists t - Ext.$ [2] $\exists t \forall x - Ext.$

St. Thomas is saying that what has the possibility of not being, might not have been (even if in fact it always was and always will be). Even a world created from all eternity might not have been, in the sense that its non-existence involves no contradiction. But this is to strain the meaning of *quandoque* and to take 'possible' as 'logically possible', which we have already seen to be wrong.

Other commentators, who agree that the *quandoque* is temporal, have disagreed whether the time St. Thomas has in mind is the time *before* the existence of the contingent being or *after* its existence. Either way it is clear that the 'is' (*est*) of 'is not' has to be taken as timeless and not significantly present-tensed. The second view seems to cohere better with the account of necessity and possibility outlined above. Throughout his proofs of the existence of God (which is supposed to be accessible to natural reason) Aquinas is anxious not to beg the question for or against creation in time (which he thought could be known only from revelation). Even of created necessary beings, it would be possible to say *quandoque non sunt* in the sense that there was a time when they were not. The special property of corruptible things like mortal animals is not that they were created in the past, it is that they will cease to exist in the future. The first part of the Third Way would indeed be superfluous on the hypothesis that the world began in time; i.e. that there was a time when there was nothing contingent in existence. If once there was nothing at all, he could argue, there would be nothing now, so there must always have been something or other; and if there was a time when there was nothing contingent then at that time there must have been something necessary. Moreover, that something, being necessary, must still and evermore exist. The reason for the steps we have been considering is to show that even if there have always been contingent beings, there cannot have been *only* contingent beings, there must have been and be at least one necessary being.

When Aquinas, in order to reduce the supposition to absurdity, supposes contingent beings to be all the beings there are, the 'are' must be taken as tenseless, as meaning 'all there are or all there ever have been'. For, from the contingency of currently existing beings, it would be obviously impossible for him to prove that everything would *by now* have ceased to exist; he could at best conclude that there *will be* some time when nothing exists, and this does not seem obviously absurd.[1]

Why should Aquinas say that whatever exists at any time with the possibility of not being, at some later time does not exist? It certainly does not seem to be a sound principle in general, that what can happen sometimes does happen. For instance, Hitler could have been assassinated; but he was not assassinated, he died at his own hand. There seem to be countless such unrealized possibilities.

Aristotle held as a general principle that whatever is always the case is necessarily the case and conversely that if something can happen it does happen some time.[2] It is difficult to know how he would have interpreted this principle in order to safeguard it against obvious counter-examples, some of which appear in his own works (e.g. the cloak which may be, but is not, cut up in *De Interpretatione* 19a 12–17).[3] In the twelfth chapter of his *De Caelo* I, he applies his axiom to corruptibility, and argues that what can corrupt at some time does corrupt.[4]

[1] It is, of course, true that if it is at any time the case that there are only contingent beings, it is at all times the case that there are only contingent beings, since necessary beings exist at all times or at none. The hypothesis that contingent beings are all there are is therefore deductively equivalent to the hypothesis that contingent beings are all there ever have been; but as Aquinas does not spell this out, it is simpler to take him as using a timeless verb in *omnia quae sunt*.

[2] The evidence for this in his works, with some speculations about his reasons for holding it, is presented in Hintikka (1) and (2).

[3] Perhaps, as Hintikka suggests, the principle was meant to apply only to kinds of things or kinds of events, not to individual things or individual events.

[4] Aristotle's arguments have been carefully examined, and found wanting, in C. J. F. Williams.

Aquinas in his commentary on the *De Caelo* writes thus. 'Someone might object to Aristotle's reasoning as follows. Let us suppose that there is something which always exists, but in such a way that its everlasting existence is contingent and not necessary. With respect then to each of the parts of the infinite time in which it is supposed to exist for ever, it will have the possibility of not existing; and it will not follow [as Aristotle had argued] that something will be simultaneously in existence and not in existence. For the case seems to be the same with the whole of an infinite period of time, and with the whole of a finite period of time. Suppose that someone is at home throughout a whole day, it does not follow that it is impossible for him to be not at home at any given period during the day; because he is at home all day contingently, and not out of necessity. However, we must say that the two cases are not on a par. For whatever exists for ever, i.e. during an infinite time, has the power of existing for an infinite time. But a power of existing is not an indifferent power with respect to the time at which one can exist, for all things tend to exist, and everything exists as much as it can'. (In I *De Caelo* XII, 258).[1]

As an exegesis of Aristotle, as Williams has pointed out, this passage is inaccurate, if charitable: in context the

---

[1] Sic igitur posset aliquis obviare rationi Aristotelis. Ponamus enim aliquid semper ens, ita tamen quod istud esse suum sempiternum sit contingens et non necessarium. Poterit ergo non esse respectu cuiuscumque partis temporis infiniti, in quo ponitur semper esse: nec propter hoc sequitur quod aliquid sit simul ens et non ens. Eadem enim ratio videtur in toto infinito tempore, et in aliquo toto tempore finito. Etsi enim ponamus quod aliquis sit in domo semper per totam diem, tamen non est impossibile eum in domo non esse in quacumque parte diei, quia non ex necessitate est in domo per totam diem sed contingenter. Sed dicendum est quod non est eadem ratio utrobique. Nam illud quod semper est, scilicet per infinitum tempus, habet potentiam ut sit in infinito tempore: potentia autem existendi non est ad utrumque respectu temporis in quo quis potest esse; omnia enim appetunt esse, et unumquodque tantum est quantum potest esse (In *De Caelo* I, XII, 258).

arguments in the *De Caelo* are supposed to depend on general logical considerations about possibility, and there is no suggestion of the principle *omnia appetunt esse*. But we are interested not in Aristotelean exegesis, but in the light this passage may throw on the Third Way.

Earlier, we saw that the Third Way was operating with a notion not of logical possibility, but of power. Is that what Aquinas is here distinguishing from logical possibility? If we take him to be doing so, we get an odd result. He says that the possibility of being (existing) which things have is one which is exercised to the full: everything exists at every moment at which it can exist. Now if the possibility of *not* existing which corruptible beings always have is a power of the same kind, then they fail to exist at every moment at which they can fail to exist; i.e. they never exist. If Aquinas is not to be led to this absurd conclusion, the power of existing he is here talking about must be a power of a different kind from the one attributed to corruptible beings in the Third Way. And this is indeed so. In the passage just cited he says that the power is not 'an indifferent power' (*potentia ad utrumque*); in the *contra Gentiles* he says 'what has the possiblity of being . . . is in itself indifferent between two things (*aequaliter se habeat ad duo*), namely being and not being'. (ScG, I, 1). A distinction is frequently made in his works between such indifferent powers (like the power of human beings to stay at home or go out of doors) and powers which are tendencies (like the potentiality of heavy bodies to fall). In the case of the latter, but not of the former, if all the conditions necessary for the exercise of the power (e.g. being unsupported) are present, then the power cannot but be exercised.

We have, therefore, in Aquinas' apparatus at least three different sorts of 'possibility':

I logical possibility: of a triangle to be equilateral,
II natural potency: of a stone to fall,
III indifferent potency: of a man to go out of doors.

There are two problems here, one of consistency and one

of truth. First, how do we reconcile the *contra Gentiles* and the *De Caelo* commentary: is the power to exist a natural power (as the latter says) or an indifferent power (as the former says)? The answer lies in the qualification in the *De Caelo*, that the power is not an indifferent one *with respect to the time at which one can exist*. That is to say, though a contingent being has the power to exist and the power not to exist, this must be the power to exist at one time, and the power not to exist at another time; there is no time such that it has the power to exist at that time and the power not to exist at that time. Hitler, say, had the power to exist in 1944 and the power not to exist in 1946; but he did not have the power not to exist in 1944, nor the power to exist in 1946. At no time did he have either of these powers. This is not just the logical point that Hitler never had the power to both exist and not exist at the same time. Such a point could be made about indifferent potencies also: I cannot both sit and not sit at the same moment. But, Aquinas says, 'my potency is to either sit or stand at sunrise tomorrow; not to do both together, but I can either stand and not sit, or sit and not stand'.[1] It is otherwise with existence, he gives us to understand: my potency is *not* to either exist or not exist at sunrise tomorrow; if I *can* exist then, I *will*.

Now if the possibility of being in the Third Way is understood as suggested by the *De Caelo* passage, and if the possibility of not being is a possibility of the same kind as that of being, as surely it must be, then a corruptible being can cease to exist only at the time when it does cease to exist: its possibility of not being is a possibility realizable only at the time when it is actually realized. We thus avoid the absurd conclusion suggested above: only of beings capable of not existing during all the time of their existence (whatever they might be) would it be true to conclude that they would never exist at all.

---

[1] Potentia mea est ad hoc quod cras in ortu solis vel sedeam vel stem, non tamen ut utrumque sit simul, sed aequaliter possum vel stare non sedendo, vel sedere non stando (In *De Caelo* I, XII, 258).

Is the principle, *omnia appetunt esse*, true? If translated as 'all things want to exist' it sounds very odd; 'everything tends to exist' sounds more plausible and less anthropomorphic. But if it is to be acceptable, it must be taken to affirm the tendency to continue in existence of what already exists, not a tendency to come into existence of what does not exist. Even so, a difficulty remains: if not all tending is wanting, surely all wanting is tending, for Aquinas; and some things do not want to exist, for instance people who attempt suicide. This difficulty, however, can be met. One can tend to exist without wanting to, as would-be suicides indeed do: they will go on existing unless they do something about it. It is true that they want not to exist, and to this extent they tend not to exist; but 'X tends not to exist' and 'X does not tend to exist' are not equivalent. There is nothing contradictory in something's tending to exist and tending to non-exist at the same time. Whether the suicide is successful or not depends on which of the conflicting tendencies (the natural tendency of the man to go on living, or the steps he takes as a result of his desire to die) overcomes the other. To say that something has a tendency to go on existing is merely to say that if something exists at t_1 and not at t_2 some explanation of the cessation of its existence is called for. The existence of Coroner's courts is evidence of the widespread desire for such types of explanation.

The principle *omnia appetunt esse* is not, therefore, absurd, so interpreted. But however charitably interpreted, it is insufficient to establish that whatever can cease to exist does cease to exist. Aquinas' argument is a *reductio ad absurdum* of the idea that there might be something which can corrupt, but does not corrupt. If it never corrupts, he argues, then, since it does exist for ever, it has the power to exist for ever; but what has the power to exist for ever must exist for ever, since everything exists as much as it can; therefore it cannot corrupt, which contradicts the original supposition. There seem to be several fallacies in this argument, of which I will mention two.

First, it makes use of *ab esse ad posse valet consequentia*, which as we have seen holds only for logical possibility. There is no reason why there should not be something which exists for ever without its having the power to exist for ever; being perhaps kept in existence, like the Vestal Virgins' fire, by powers resident in a succession of external agents. Such a thing might very well have the power not to exist, for all Aquinas' argument shows.

Secondly, if we agree with Aquinas that everything exists as long as it can, this does not mean 'as long as it has a natural power to' but 'as long as it is not interfered with'. By an interfering agent a substance can be corrupted before the time natural for things of its kind to cease to exist, as a man can be cut off in his prime. Hence it is not true that what has the power to exist for ever necessarily does exist for ever.

Indeed if in *potentia ad esse* we have to specify the time of the *esse*, as Aquinas says, the same must be true of the *esse* in *omnia appentunt esse*; for there seems no reason why certain kinds of things should not have a natural life-span after which their cessation from existence calls for no explanation other than that they are the kinds of thing they are. Radio-active elements appear to be of this kind; to what extent human beings are is a matter of some dispute, I understand, among physiologists.

We now turn to the apparent quantifier shift in arguing from

(6) Each thing at some time or other is not

to (7) At some time or other, everything is not.

Why should not corruptible beings overlap each other, so that each one comes to be and passes away, but there is never any time when nothing at all exists? Aquinas says that on the supposition that everything is corruptible there *was* a time when nothing existed (*aliquando nihil fuit*) and we may feel inclined to query the past tense: how does he think he has shown that the time of general non-existence is in the past and not something yet to come? Presumably at the background is the supposition that the world has existed for ever.

A possibility which has not been realized in an infinite time, the argument goes, is not a real possibility; so that if the possibility of each thing in the world's corrupting involves the possibility of the whole world's corrupting, this second possibility too must have been realized by now if there has already been an infinite time. The weakness in this argument is the step from

(8) Each thing has the possibility of corrupting

to (9) There is a possibility of everything's corrupting.

This step involves a fallacy analogous to the quantifier-shift fallacy discussed above; only here the shift is not between two quantifiers, but between a quantifier and a modal operator.[1] Its fallaciousness is easily shown informally by counterexample. In a fair contest, each competitor has the possibility of winning the whole first prize; it is not possible for every competitor to win the whole first prize.

Geach has defended the Third Way against an objection similar to the one I have made. 'It is irrelevant to object to this proof that a material universe wholly composed of corruptible things might go on existing even if all its parts actually corrupted, because their matter could still exist under different forms; for the objection presupposes that this matter is not perishable as such, in the way that things composed of it are; but then this matter will itself be one of the imperishable things Aquinas is talking about at this stage of the proof.' (Geach, 115). Aquinas did indeed believe that matter was imperishable, being itself presupposed by either generation or corruption, and Geach is no doubt correct to say that someone who accepted this account of

[1] Using 'Cx' for 'x is corrupted', we have

(8) $\forall x M C x$
(9) $M \forall x C x$

Aquinas seems to use this fallacious argument at ScG III, 86. 'Ex multis contingentibus non potest fieri unum necessarium; quia sicut quodlibet contingentium per se deficere potest ab essendi, ita et omnia simul.'

matter would have to agree that there does in a sense exist an imperishable entity. But Aquinas often insists that matter and form do not really exist in the way that substances do, and the existence of imperishable matter is certainly not proved by the argument in the Third Way based on the observable facts of generation and corruption. Why should the objection presuppose, as Geach says, that matter is imperishable? It is true that if there is to be change as distinct from succession, there must be something common to the two terms of the change. If A turns into B and is not just replaced by B then there must be something common to both A and B, and this is precisely what is meant by matter's being presupposed by generation and corruption. Similarly if B then turns into C, there must be something in common between them. But why need there be anything in common between A and C? What was common between A and B may have ceased to exist before there began to exist what is in common between A and B. To argue from

(10) In every change there must be a common element between the terms of the change,

to (11) There must be some element common to the terms of every change

is to commit yet another quantifier-shift fallacy.

Of course many people who would not accept Thomas' hylomorphism would accept some principle of conservation of matter: atomists, for instance, both ancient and modern. And in certain scientific theories there may be good reasons to postulate such a conservation. But no such principle is here proved by Aquinas; and it can be denied by an objector without any violation of the principle that nothing comes out of nothing.

It might be argued that a universe composed of perishable beings might itself be regarded as a necessary being. Certainly, a universe composed of temporal beings might itself be everlasting. But Aquinas, as we have seen, held it impossible that many contingent things might make one necessary being; and though he failed to prove this impossibility the impossibility of an everlasting but contingent universe seems equally unproven.

Aquinas now goes on to argue that if there had once been nothing, there would now be nothing, because nothing can be brought into existence by nothing. The principle to which he here appeals differs from the maxim quoted above, that nothing comes from, or out of, nothing. Aquinas did not accept this maxim, though Aristotle did; for Aquinas, unlike Aristotle, believed that the whole world had come from nothing: it had been created, *out of* nothing, *by* God. Hume, on the other hand, argued that it was possible for something to come into existence not only from nothing, but also by nothing; not only without matter, but also without a cause.

The difference between Aquinas and Hume here appears to be parallel to that between steady-rate theorists and proponents of the big bang theory among recent scientific cosmologists. According to the big bang theory, the whole matter of the universe began to exist at a particular time in the remote past. A proponent of such a theory, at least if he is an atheist, must believe that the matter of the universe came from nothing and by nothing. A steady state theorist, however, while believing that the matter of the universe comes *from* nothing, need not believe that it has no cause. Hoyle, for instance, writes as follows while explaining how new material appears in space to compensate for the background material which is constantly being condensed into galaxies. 'At one time created atoms do not exist, at a later time they do. The creation arises from a field which you must think of as generated by the matter which exists already . . . matter that already exists causes new matter to appear' (Hoyle, 110). Like Aquinas, and unlike Hume, Hoyle thinks that the origination of matter calls for a cause. But like Aristotle, and unlike Aquinas, he thinks that there has always been matter.

If one could establish without appeal to revelation that the material world had not always existed, then the principle that no substance can begin to exist without a cause would provide a swift proof of a Creator. What is the status of this principle, which Aquinas asserted and Hume denied? I do not know that the principle has ever been established, nor how one would set out to do so; on the other hand, it does not seem to have been refuted, though Hume is popularly credited with doing so. It is, says Hume, 'easy for us to conceive any object to be non-existent this moment, and existent the next, without conjoining to it the distinct idea of a cause or productive principle. The separation, therefore, of the idea of a cause from that of a beginning of existence, is plainly possible for the imagination; and consequently the actual separation of these objects is so far possible, that it implies no contradiction nor absurdity' (Treatise, I, III, III). There are two fallacies here: first, the possibility of conceiving A without conceiving B does not imply the possibility of conceiving (A without B): I can conceive of air without conceiving of oxygen, but I cannot conceive of air without oxygen, at least in any sense in which conceiving of this would imply the possibility of there actually being air without oxygen. Secondly, the step from

(12) There is no cause which is necessary for any particular beginning of existence,

to (13) Any particular beginning of existence needs no cause

is once again the result of a fallacious shifting of modal operators;[1] and once again the fallacy can be brought out by a counterexample. There is no one wife who is necessary to make a particular man a husband (Henry VIII and others have shown this) but it does not follow that a man does not need to have a wife in order to become a husband.[2]

The principle does not, however, have in the Third Way

---

[1] Let 'Bx' be 'x begins to exist', 'Pxy' be 'x brings y into existence', 'Lp' be 'necessarily p'.

(12) $-\forall y(By \rightarrow \exists x\, LPxy)$
(13) $-AyL(By \rightarrow \exists x\, Pxy)$

[2] The fallaciousness of Hume's argument was pointed out by Miss Anscombe in Anscombe (1), p. 188.

the importance which it has for Hume, since Aquinas'
argument is meant to be probative even if the world had no
beginning. The concluding stage of his argument turns on
the distinction between caused and uncaused necessary
beings. He frequently explains this distinction by means of
a geometrical illustration meant to show that even something
which is everlasting may be causally dependent. 'It is clear
that a triangle always has its three angles equal to two right
angles; but of this perpetual fact there is something else
which is the cause. But there are other perpetual things
which have no other cause, such as first principles.'[1] The
sense of 'cause' used here has to be one which includes the
'because' of *a priori* disciplines; and the dependence involved is the kind of dependence which later steps of an
argument have on earlier steps. This amalgamation of
causal and logical dependence seems to involve a misunder-
standing of the nature of axiomatic systems. One need not
be a conventionalist to think that whether a particular thesis
is 'dependent' or 'independent' is relative to the system
chosen. A necessary truth which appears as a theorem in
one system may appear as an axiom in another, and vice
versa. This makes logical dependence too unlike the causal
relationship which Aquinas seeks to establish between God
and an everlasting world.

If Hume were right that the notion of temporal priority
was an essential element in the notion of cause, then it would
be senseless to speak of something caused *ab eterno*. But
Hume seems to be wrong. Surely, it is a contingent fact that
light takes time to travel; and before this fact was discovered
it was perfectly possible to distinguish the source of illumination from the object illuminated. Consequently, in spite
of the infelicity of Aquinas' example, there does not seem
anything obviously incoherent in the idea that the world
might be everlasting and yet caused. Yet the concluding

[1] Manifestum est enim quod triangulus semper habet tres angulos
aequales duobus rectis; sed tamen huius perpetuae passionis est altera
causa. Sed aliqua perpetua sunt, sicut principa, quorum non est altera
causa. *In Physic.* VIII, 3.

section of the Third Way quite fails to show it *must* be caused, and by a creator.

The argument goes: there are everlasting beings; these must be caused or uncaused; they cannot all be caused; so there must be an uncaused everlasting being, which is God. In order to show that not all the everlasting beings can be uncaused, Aquinas refers back to his earlier regress argument, and we can refer back to its refutation.[1] In order to show that the uncaused everlasting being must be God, he offers no proof, and we may ask why might it not be perpetual, indestructible matter? If the first part of the Third Way has any force at all, the matter of an everlasting world would be matter with a natural power of everlasting existence. And what better explanation could one want of an everlasting existence than a natural power for everlasting existence? In what way would God's eternal existence be more self-explanatory than the everlasting existence of matter with a natural indestructibility? A difference between the two, it seems, could only be made out by saying that God's perpetual existence would be logically necessary, that of Aristotelean matter would be only naturally necessary. But that would take us from the Third Way into the Leibnizian argument from contingency; and it would vindicate Kant's criticism that the cosmological argument for God's existence must ultimately depend upon the ontological one.

[1] See p. 24 above.

5

The Fourth Way

The Fourth Way is based on the gradation found in things. Some things are discovered to be more or less good, or true, or noble, than other things, and so on. But things are said to be more or less F to the extent to which they approach to something which is most F; for example, things are hotter the more they approach what is hottest. There is therefore something which is truest and best and noblest of things, and consequently most in being (*maxime ens*); for Aristotle says that the truest things are the things most in being. Now whatever is most F is the cause of whatever else is F, just as fire (as Aristotle says in the same book) is the hottest thing and the cause of all other hot things. Therefore there is something which causes being and goodness and any perfection in all things; and this we call 'God'.[1]

[1] Quarta via sumitur ex gradibus qui in rebus inveniuntur. Invenitur enim in rebus aliquid magis et minus bonum et verum et nobile, et sic de aliis hujusmodi. Sed magis et minus dicitur de diversis secundum quod appropinquant diversimode ad aliquid quod maxime est; sicut magis calidum est quod magis appropinquat maxime calido. Est igitur aliquid quod est verissimum et optimum et nobilissimum et per consequens maxime ens; nam quae sunt maxime vera sunt maxime entia, ut dicitur II *Metaph. Quod* autem *dicitur maxime in aliquo genere est causa omnium quae sunt illius generis,* sicut *ignis qui est maxime calidus est causa omnium calidorum,* ut in eodem libro dicitur. Ergo est aliquid quod est causa esse et bonitatis et cujuslibet perfectionis in omnibus rebus, et hoc dicimus Deum.

Admirers of Aquinas are divided in their attitude to the Fourth Way. Some, such as Geach, suspect it of being indefensible; others, such as Gilson, say that 'the fourth way can be said to be the deepest one from the point of view of metaphysical knowledge' (Gilson, 76). All agree, however, that it is the way in which, for better or worse, St. Thomas comes closest to Platonism. I shall begin this chapter, therefore, with a sketch of Plato's Theory of Ideas or Forms.[1]

Plato's theory arises as follows. Peter, James and John are each called 'human'; they have it in common that they are all human. Now when we say 'Peter is human' does the word 'human' stand for something in the way that the word 'Peter' stands for the individual man Peter? If so, what? Is it the same thing as the word 'human' stands for in the sentence 'Paul is human'? Plato's answer is yes: in each case in which such an expression occurs it stands for the same thing, namely, that because of which Peter and Paul are each human. This is given various designations by Plato, corresponding for instance to 'the human itself', 'that very thing which is human', and — by analogy with other cases — 'humanity'. But its best known designation is 'The Idea or Form of the human'.

In many cases where we would say that a common predicate was true of a number of individuals Plato will say that they are all related to a certain Form of Idea: where A, B, C. are all F, they are related to a single Form of F. It is not clear how universally Plato applied this principle. Sometimes he states it universally, at other times he hesitates about applying it to certain particular sorts of predicate. Certainly he lists ideas of many different types, such as the idea of good, the idea of bed, the idea of circle, the idea of being, the idea of sameness. Again, he is prepared to extend the theory beyond single-place predicates such as '. . . is human'

---

[1] The account given below is partly controversial. Since we are not concerned here with Platonic exegesis, I have not given references to justifying texts, nor discussed the development of Plato's thought. The interested reader may pursue the matter in chapter three of Wedberg, to whose exposition I am greatly indebted.

to two-place predicates like '. . . is distinct from . . .'. In the *Parmenides*, for instance, he says that when we say that A is distinct from B and when we say that B is distinct from A, although we use the word 'distinct' twice, each time we are applying it 'to that nature of which it is the name'. As long as he held the theory at all Plato seems to have believed in the Ideas of good and noble and being. It is these which are relevant to the argument in the Fourth Way.

We may state a number of Platonic theses about Ideas and their relations to particulars.

(1) Wherever several things are F, this is because they participate or imitate a single Idea of F

(2) No Idea is a participant or imitator of itself

(3) (*a*) The Idea of F is F

(*b*) The Idea of F is nothing but F

(4) Nothing but the Idea of F is really and truly altogether F

(5) Ideas are not in space or time, they have no parts and do not change, they are not perceptible to the senses.

Theses (1), (2) and (3) make up an inconsistent triad, which gives rise to a well-known difficulty about the Theory of Ideas. The antinomy was first expounded by Plato himself in the Third Man argument in the *Parmenides*, where he argues as follows. Let us suppose we have a number of particulars each of which is F. Then, by (1), there is an Idea of F. This, by (3), is itself F. But now the Idea of F and the original F things make up a new collection of F things. By (1) again, this must be because they participate in an Idea of F. But, by (2), this cannot be the Idea first postulated. So there must be another Idea of F; but this in its turn, by (3), will be F; and so on *ad infinitum*. So, against (1), there will be not a single Idea but infinitely many. This antinomy was never resolved by Plato; it is still a matter of dispute between scholars whether he shrugged it off or abandoned all or part of his theory as a consequence.[1]

---

[1] See, for instance, chapters IV, XII, XIII, XIV in Allen.

Thesis (4) is sometimes stated in a misleading way by commentators. Plato frequently says that only Ideas really are, and that the non-ideal particulars we encounter in sense-experience are between being and not being. He is often taken to be saying that only Ideas really exist, and that tangible objects are unreal and illusory. In context, it is clear that when Plato says that only Ideas really are, he does not mean that only Ideas really exist, but that only the Idea of F is really F, whatever F may be in the particular case. Particulars are between being and not being in that they are between being F and not being F—i.e. they are sometimes F and sometimes not F, or they are F in some respects and not in others. For instance, only the Idea of beauty is really beautiful, because particular beautiful things are (1) beautiful in one respect and ugly in another (say, in figure but not complexion); or (2) beautiful at one time but not another (e.g. at the age of 20 but not at 70); or (3) beautiful by comparison with some things, not by comparison with others (e.g. Miss England may be beautiful by comparison with Miss Blackpool but ugly by comparison with Miss World); (4) beautiful in some surroundings, not in others.[1]

With regard to thesis (5) I will say merely that it attributes to Ideas properties which Aquinas, and a long theological tradition, attribute to God.

The problem to which Plato's theory is an inadequate solution is sometimes called the problem of universals. In contemporary discussion of this problem, four notions can be discerned which bear some resemblance to Plato's Ideas.

(*A*) W. V. O. Quine has suggested that in a sentence such as 'water in fluid' 'water' can be treated as the name of a single scattered object, the aqueous part of the world, made up out of puddles, rivers, lakes and so on (Quine (2), 98). It has sometimes been thought—though not by Quine (Quine (1), 68)—that the meaning of 'water' when it occurs in predicate place—as in 'that puddle is water'—could be similarly explained: the predicate, on this view, would stand

---

[1] Here I follow Vlastos, 11–12.

for a concrete universal. Such a concrete universal would have a certain similarity with Plato's Ideas. It would explain Plato's preference (not always shared by his commentators) for referring to his Ideas by a concrete mode of speech (e.g. 'the beautiful') rather than an abstract one ('beauty'). It would give a clear sense to his theory that particulars participate in Ideas: this particular pool of water is quite literally a part of all-the-water-in-the-universe. Corresponding to thesis (2) is the fact that the concrete universal is not a proper part of itself. As for (3*a*), obviously all the water in the universe is water; and as for (4), nothing but the Idea of water is all the water there is. However, a concrete universal is very unlike a Platonic Idea in respect of (5)—the water in the universe can be located and can change in quantity and distribution, it can be seen and touched. Hence (3*b*) is also false; the concrete universal has many other properties besides that of being water.

(*B*) Wittgenstein, followed by others, has suggested that Platonic forms might be looked on as paradigms or standards: the relation between particulars and Ideas is similar to that between particular metre-long objects and the Standard Metre in Paris.[1] This brings out well the imitation and resemblance aspect of Plato's theory: to be a metre long is, precisely, to resemble in length the Standard Metre; and if two things are each a metre long it is in virtue of this common resemblance to the paradigm. An object like the Standard Metre is not naturally thought of as resembling itself, and this fits with (2); yet the standard metre is undoubtedly one metre long, if anything is, which fits (3*a*). Like a concrete universal, a paradigm object fits those aspects of Plato's ideas which make them seem substantial entities; like a concrete universal, it fails to have the properties by which Platonic Ideas transcend the sensible world. The Standard Metre is not in heaven but in Paris, and is discerned not by intellectual vision but by the eyes in one's head.

[1] See Geach (2), 267.

(*C*) Modern logicians sometimes speak of attributes (which Frege called 'concepts'), such as humanity, or the property of being divisible by seven. These abstract entities share the more transcendental properties of Plato's ideas: humanity does not grow or die as human beings do, and nowhere in the world could one view or handle divisibility by seven. All men, we might say, are human by virtue of sharing a common humanity; this humanity, we might say, is the concept for which the predicate '. . . is human' stands for in the sentences 'Peter is human' and 'Paul is human'. But if we think of Platonic ideas in this way as attributes, it is very hard to see how Plato could ever have come to believe in (3) and (4): how could he have thought that humanity itself, and only humanity itself, was really a human being? Is it not clear that humanity is an abstraction, and that only a concrete individual can be a human being?

(*D*) Attributes serve as principles according to which objects can be collected into classes: objects which possess the attribute of humanity, for instance, can be grouped into the class of human beings. In some ways classes seem closer than attributes to Platonic ideas: participation in an idea can be understood without too much difficulty as membership of a class. Classes, like attributes, and unlike paradigms and concrete universals, resemble Ideas in their abstract properties. Classes, however, unlike attributes, are extensional entities: two classes with the same members are identical, whereas attribute A need not be identical with attribute B though all and only those who possess A possess also B. Being a man, for instance, is not being a featherless biped, though the class of featherless bipeds may well be the same as the class of men. It is not clear whether Plato's Ideas are extensional like classes or non-extensional like attributes.[1] The difficulty in identifying Ideas with classes arises over theses (2) and (3). The class of men is not a man and we cannot say in general that the class of Fs is F; some classes are members of themselves and some are not. Notoriously,

[1] See Wedberg, 31, 35.

the class of classes which are not members of themselves gives rise to paradoxes, as Russell discovered: if this class is a member of itself it is not a member of itself; and if it is not a member of itself then it is a member of itself. Though Platonic Ideas cannot be identified with classes, the kinship between them is great enough for it to be no accident that Russell's paradox bears a striking resemblance to the Third Man argument in the *Parmenides*.

Concepts such as those of attributes and class are more or less sophisticated descendants of Plato's notion; none of them, however, does justice to the many facets of his Ideas. If one wants to see how the theses (1) to (5) seemed plausible to Plato, it is better not to take a logician's technical concept, but some more unreflective notion. Consider for example a point of the compass, not as one might try to explain it in virtue of an abstract notion e.g., eastwardness, but as one might conceive it by naively reflecting on the various locutions we use e.g. about the East. There are many places which are East of us, e.g. Belgrade, Warsaw, and Peking. Anything which is thus East is in The East, is indeed a part of The East (participation); or, if you prefer, it is in more or less the same direction as The East (imitation). It is by virtue of being in The East, or by virtue of being in the same direction as that point of the compass, that whatever is east of us is east. (Thesis (1).) Now The East cannot be identified with any of the places which are east: it is provincial to think that 'The East' means a place such as India; since from some other point of view, e.g. Peking, India is part of the West. (Thesis (2).) The East itself, of course, is east of us — to walk towards The East you must walk eastwards — and it is nothing but east: we may say 'The East is red', but we really mean that the eastern *sky* is red. (Thesis (3).) Nothing but The East is unqualifiedly east: the sun is sometimes east and sometimes west, India is east of Iran but west of Vietnam and so on; but in every time and every place The East is east. (Thesis (4).) Moreover, The East cannot be identified with any point in space, nor has it any history in time, nor can it be seen, handled, or parcelled out. (Thesis (5).)

I am not, of course, suggesting that points of the compass will supply an interpretation of Plato's Ideas which will make all theses (1) to (5) come out true. No interpretation could do this since the theses are not all compatible with each other. I am merely saying that this interpretation will make the theses look *prima facie* plausible in a way in which the interpretations previously considered will not. If one is to make sense of what we say about the East, it is better to take the sentences in which the expression occurs and translate them into sentences which concern rather the relation of *being to the east of*, and the classes that can be picked out by this attribute. Attributes and classes, of course, have their own difficulties, as the history of the philosophy of logic since Frege shows. We have yet to answer Plato's problems; but we cannot go back to his solution.

Aquinas' relationship to Plato's theory of Ideas is difficult to define. On the one hand, he frequently takes up an explicitly anti-Platonic stance; on the other, he sometimes seems to make an implicit appeal to the theory. Plato, he said, was mistaken in positing separate Ideas of natural species, such as an absolute man and an absolute horse.[1] Sometimes, however, he speaks as if two men, such as Peter and Paul, have one and the same humanity (e.g. Ia 3 art 5); elsewhere he explains that the essence or form signified by the name 'human', namely humanity, is really divided in different individuals, so that the unity of human nature is not real but notional, the humanity of Peter being numerically distinct from the humanity of Paul.[2] On this view the

---

[1] I a, 6, 4 c Plato . . . ponebat ideam hominis et equi separatam, quam vocabat per se hominem et per se equum . . . haec opinio irrationabilis videtur quantum ad hoc, quod ponebat species rerum naturalium separatas per se subsistentes.

[2] Ia 39 ed ad 3: forma significata per hoc nomen homo, id est humanitas, realiter dividitur in diversis suppositis . . . unitas autem sive communitas humanae naturae non est secundum rem, sed solum secundum considerationem. *In I Sent*, d 2, q 1 a 4: alia humanitas est numero in Socrate et Platone. I am indebted to Mr. Geach for the former reference.

predicate in 'Peter is human' will not stand for any substance
like a concrete universal, nor for a universal abstraction
such as humanity, but rather for a particular, individualized,
essence, the humanity of Peter, which will have a history of
its own, unlike a Platonic Idea. Similarly, in 'Socrates is
wise' the predicate will stand for an individualized form, the
wisdom of Socrates. This form will be an accidental form,
unlike the humanity of Socrates; for Socrates can exist without being wise, though he cannot exist without being
human.[1]

There are a number of difficulties in this theory of individualized forms: one is that if 'Socrates is wise' is false,
there is no such thing as the wisdom of Socrates for the
predicate to stand for, and so the introduction of the forms
does not help to explain how the predicate has meaning.
But the theory can at least be explained without committing
its holder to Platonism; and it has recently been well expounded in this manner by Geach. The form which is re-
ferred to by the predicate of 'Socrates is wise' may be re-
ferred to also by the phrase 'the wisdom of Socrates'; but
this latter expression must not be construed as 'Wisdom,
which stands in the special relation *belonging to* to Socrates',
just as 'the square root of four' does not mean 'The Square
Root, which stands in a special relation to four'. 'Wisdom,
tout court, means nothing in heaven or earth; wisdom is
always wisdom-of — as Aquinas puts it, it is of-something
(*entis*) rather than itself something (*ens*)' (Geach 3, 78).

There is, however, in Aquinas' theory a Platonism at the
second remove. On Aquinas' view, we have seen, it is not
strictly correct to say that Peter and Paul are both human
because they share a common humanity; for the humanity of
Peter is not identical with the humanity of Paul. But suppose
we go on to ask: what makes the humanity of Peter and the
humanity of Paul both humanities? Aquinas' answer is that
they are both individuations and determinations of the same

---

[1] See IIIa, 17, 2. Some passages in Plato himself suggest a doctrine
of individualized accidental forms (e.g., Phaedo 102 d 7).

common nature: and for this to make sense, the common
nature must be extra-mental like a Platonic Idea.[1] To be
sure, he does not think there exists in the world an unindi-
viduated humanity; but this is not because, as on Geach's
view, there would be something absurd, or ill-formed, in an
expression denoting such an unindividualized essence.
Rather, an unindividualized form in Aquinas' system plays
the part which motion on a frictionless surface plays in
Galileo's dynamics. There are no frictionless surfaces in the
world, but the actual motions of bodies are to be explained
as deviations from the motions they would have if the surfaces on which they move were frictionless. Similarly, there
are no unindividualized specific forms, but an explanation is
needed why the forms there are individualized. Thus
Aquinas says 'Forms, considered in themselves, are common
to many things; it is because they are received in matter,
that they become forms of particular things'.[2] And in the
very passage from the *Summa* which contains his explicit
repudiation of Platonism, he goes on to explain that the individual goodnesses of things are all likenesses of the divine
goodness, which is the first paradigm of all goodness
(Ia 6, 4c). The relationship of these individualized forms to
the divine goodness is the same as that which Plato posited
between particular goods and the Idea of Good.

Nowhere is the vestigial Platonism of Aquinas more
crucial than in the Fourth Way. The argument starts from
the existence of multiple, limited, individualized forms, and
proceeds towards a single perfect entity with the properties
of an Idea. 'Some things are discovered to be more or less
good, or true, or noble, than other things, and so on.
But things are said to be more or less F to the extent to
which they approach to something which is most F; for

[1] Cf. e.g. *In I Sent*, d 24 q 1 a 1: oportet quod sit aliquod materiale
per quod natura communis individuatur et determinatis ad hoc
singulare.

[2] Ia 7, 1c Forma, in se considerata, communis est ad multa; sed
per hoc quod recipitur in materia fit forma determinata.

example things are hotter the more they approach what is hottest.'

In one way, the starting point here is unexceptionable. 'Some things are better than others' is certainly correct if all this means is that some propositions of the form 'A is better than B' are acceptable. But there is a difficulty about a scale of goodness which is quite unconnected with Platonism. Some people would question whether the varieties of goodness are 'a gradation to be found in things' at all; grading, they would say, is rather something we do to things, an activity whose characteristic vehicle is a commendatory utterance such as 'this is good' which is not helpfully regarded as having a truth-value. But even if we reject this view, and regard it as a matter of objective fact whether something is a good F or not, it still does not seem possible to order good things on a single scale of goodness as we can arrange hot things on a single scale of temperature. Something may, for instance, be a good F and a bad G (as a man may be a good cricketer and a bad husband); and it is not obvious how we can settle whether good Fs are better or worse, in any unqualified sense, then good Gs (is a good hippopotamus better or worse than a good sunset?). If we want to find whether anything is good or not, we must specify what kind of thing it is, and what aspects or purpose we have in mind; 'good' *tout court* is too schematic a word for anything like a precise scale of goodness to seem a possibility.

One way in which Aquinas seems to envisage a scale of 'goodness' or 'nobility' is a scale of ascending cognitive powers. Thus, in the course of an argument to prove that God possesses cognition, he writes 'What is found in many things in a greater or lesser degree according to the degree of their approach to something else, must be found to the greatest degree in that something else; as heat is found to the greatest degree in fire, and other non-elementary bodies are hotter the nearer they approach to fire. Now we find that the nearer things are to the first principle, the more noble a share they have in cognition; as men have a greater share than brutes, and angels more than men; so that in God there must be found the noblest cognition of all.'[1]

In this passage and in the Fourth Way there is a problem about the notion of approaching a maximum. Is the maximum (of heat, or of goodness) supposed to be something ideal (the hottest possible thing, the best possible thing) or something actual (the hottest actual thing, the best actual thing)? If the former, then it seems plausible to identify the best thing with God; but the degrees of goodness in no way seem to show the actual existence of any best possible thing, any more than degrees of size show that there exists a largest possible thing. If the latter, then the existence of things of varying degrees of goodness will show that there exists a *de facto* best thing (at least in the sense of a thing than which there is no better): but why should this be God rather than, say, a good man? It is at this point that St. Thomas needs to appeal implicitly to Plato to fill the gap; for on Plato's view, to be more or less F precisely is to participate more or less fully in the Idea of F which is the most F thing, the one and only thing which is fully F.[2]

---

[1] Quod invenitur in pluribus magis et minus secundum quod plures alicui appropinquant oportet ut in illo maxime inveniantur; sicut calor in igne, ad quam quanto corpora mixta magis accedunt, calidiora sunt. Invenitur autem quod quanto aliqua magis accedant ad primum, nobilius cognitionem participant; sicut homines plus quam bruta et angeli magis homines; unde oportet quod in Deo nobillissima cognitio inveniatur (*In I Sent* d. 35 q. 1. a. 1).

[2] We might ask, as Wedberg does, why Plato does not regard a thing which is say very hot as participating in form of being very hot, while a thing which is fairly hot participates in a form of being fairly hot; this he thinks would be more in accord with a thoroughgoing Platonic realism which posited a form to correspond with every predicate. The answer is probably that Plato was operating with a fairly loose criterion of identity for predicates according to which 'is fairly hot' and 'is very hot' would be instances of the same predicate. Certainly he seems to count 'is beautiful by comparison with a pig' and 'is beautiful by comparison with Aphrodite' as instances of the same predicate.

The most interesting part of the Platonism of the Fourth Way is the application which Aquinas makes of it to the predicate *ens*. The thing, he says, which is truest and best and noblest is, by consequence, the most being of things. This predicate *ens* was a scholastic coinage from the Latin verb 'to be', *esse*; and *esse*, said Aquinas, was the activity of *ens* as shining was the activity of what shines (*In III Sent* d 6 q 2 a 2).

To understand Aquinas' theory of *esse* we have to consider the way in which he distinguishes it from form or essence. In his youthful work *De Ente et Essentia* he introduces the distinction in the following manner: Every essence can be understood without anything being known about its actual existence (*esse*); for I can understand what a man is, or what a phoenix is, without knowing whether these things exist (*esse habeant*) in reality (*in rerum natura*); so it is obvious that existence (*esse*) is different from a thing's essence, i.e. what the thing is (its *quidditas*) (*De Ente*, V.). The distinction here made is clear enough, and familiar in modern philosophy in different terminologies. I can understand a predicate without knowing whether it is true of anything; can grasp a concept without knowing whether it has application; can use the expression '. . . is a phoenix' without knowing whether anything is a phoenix. *Esse*, so explained, seems well translated by 'existence' as this is represented in modern logic by the existential quantifier. But if we understand *esse* in this way it is impossible to make sense of what Aquinas also says in this work, namely that God is subsistent *esse*, that his essence is his *esse*, and (ch. VI) that he is pure *esse* to which no addition can be made. For this would mean that God was subsistent existence, that to know that He exists is the same as to know what He is, and that God's essence was best represented by an existential quantifier followed by a bound variable but no predicate.

No one in recent years has defended Aquinas' account of *esse* more vigorously than Geach; but Geach admits that the *De Ente* theory is untenable and brings out its nonsensicality by the following dialogue:

Theist: There is a God.

Atheist: So you say: but what sort of being is this God of yours?

Theist: Why I've just told you: There *is* a God, that's what God is!

Geach argues, however, that Aquinas abandoned this nonsensical view in his later work. He fails, however, to establish this change of mind about *esse*. Let us consider the texts he offers in support of his claim.[1] First he says: 'The clearest ones relate to the 'existence' of privations like blindness. Blindness is not an *ens* and has no *esse*; for it is not among the things that are, being on the contrary precisely the absence of what would be an existing thing, viz. the absence of sight from an eye. All the same, we can truly say that there is blindness in a given eye, which is an affirmative answer to an '*an est*'? question. Thus the existence asserted in this case by saying 'there is . . .' is quite different from Aquinas' *esse* (Ia 48 art 2 ad 2m).

In several places, certainly, Aquinas follows Aristotle in distinguishing between two senses of *esse*. In one sense it applies to things belonging in one or other of the ten Aristotelean categories; in the other it is merely a *verbalis copula*.[2] Privations, Aquinas says, *are* in the second sense: 'it is said that blindness *is* in the second sense, insofar as the proposition 'something is blind' is true; but it *is* not in the first sense, for it has no *esse* in reality but is rather the privation of an *esse*'.

Three observations, however, are in order. First, this is not an anticipation of the modern quantifier, as Geach seems to think; for what Aquinas would translate into 'Something is a phoenix' is not 'a phoenix exists' but 'phoenixhood exists'. Secondly, these passages are not evidence of a change of mind. Already in the *De Ente* we read '*ens* is used in two senses: in the first it can be divided into the ten

---

[1] Geach (3), 88–90.

[2] Cf. for instance, *In Meta*, V, 1, 9, 896; *De Pot*, VII, 2; *Quodl.* 9, 3.

categories; in the second it signifies the truth of a proposition. In the second sense everything about which an affirmative proposition can be formed can be called *ens*, even though it supposes nothing in reality; in this way privations and negations are called *entia*; thus we say that an affirmation *is* the opposite of a negation, and that . . . blindness is in an eye . . . but in the first sense blindness and the like are not *entia*' (*De Ente*, 1).

Thirdly, it is true that this analysis is applied by Aquinas to privations other than blindness — e.g. to evil in 1a, 60, 2, 2. But it would be wrong to think that Aquinas offers a general account of existential statements according to which the apparent subject of any such statement is to be replaced by a logical predicate, as it is in modern quantifier analysis. This comes out if we consider the second of Geach's texts.

'At Ia. 3, 4 ad 2m' Geach says 'Aquinas actually uses the obvious difference in meaning that there would be between a statement that there is a God and a statement of what God is, as a *prima facie* objection to the doctrine that God's *esse* and nature are identical. His reply to this objection is that to know (by reason of a proof) that there is a God is not to apprehend God's *esse*: God's *esse* and his nature are alike beyond our knowledge in this life; and as a positive account of the assertion that there is a God, he tells us that this 'existence' is the truth of an affirmative predication (*compositio*). 'God exists' is true if and only if *the term 'God'* is affirmatively predicatable.'

But there is no suggestion in the passage quoted from Aquinas that *Deus* functions as a predicate in '*Deus est*'; on the contrary this proposition is consistently treated as a subject-predicate one.[1] The subject term stands for God, the predicate term *est* for God's *esse*; if we fully understood the subject term (i.e. if we saw God's essence) we would see that it stood for the same thing as the predicate stands for; but in this life we need proof, or faith, to convince us that

---

[1] See *De Pot*, VII, 2 ad 11; ScG 1, 10 (3) and 11 (ad 3).

the predicate applies to the subject. This passage of Aquinas, therefore, does not seem to deserve credit for setting forth a principle which 'will enable us to steer through all the shoals of the Cartesian Ontological Argument'.

Geach's third text, *Quodl.* IX, 3, is the one which seems to come closest to anticipating the quantifier analysis. This question discusses the Catholic doctrine that Christ always existed as God, but began to exist as a human being; and it asks: are there, in Christ, two *esses* or just one? Aquinas replies that there is only one; but as an objection to this he says: If you can ask of a thing *an est?* then you can attribute *esse* to it. But you can ask *an est?* of Christ's human nature; so it has an *esse* distinct from that of its divine nature. He replies to this objection that it uses esse in the sense in which to say that a thing *is* is merely to say that true propositions can be formed of it; and in this sense *esse* belongs to any *ens* and even to non*entia* such as blindness. Here we seem to be told that the blindness analysis can be applied not only to privation but also to *entia* which have real *esse*, such as a human nature.

But even this does not involve an analysis of existative propositions similar to a quantifier. The part of the blindness analysis which can be applied to all terms whatever, is simply that part which states '*X est*' = '*Affirmativa propositio potest formari de X*'. But the part of the blindness analysis which, as we saw, is not applied to God, and, as we shall see, is not applied to any kind of substance, is that the affirmative proposition is one in which the term X appears not in subject place but in predicate place.

There is a distinction, Aquinas explains, among the things which have *esse* in Aristotle's second sense, as items under one or other category. Where the X in question is not a complete substance, but a form, then the proposition '*X est*' will be analysed in the same way as for privations: to attribute *esse* to the wisdom of Socrates is to say that Socrates is wise (*est sapientia Socrates = Socrates est sapiens*) (*Quodl.* IX, 3). But when the X in question is a complete substance, the proposition whose truth is asserted by the

proposition '*X est*' is that proposition itself; and though, as
we shall see, this proposition is capable of further analysis,
it is not capable of any analysis which shifts the 'X' from
subject-place. Consequently, it is not because they are
existential propositions that '*caecitas est*' and '*sapientia est*'
are analysed in the switching-round way characteristic of the
quantifier; it is because they are propositions whose subjects
are not complete substances. The texts cited by Geach,
then, do not establish that Aquinas revised his theory of
esse.

Aquinas changed his mind, it seems to me, not so much
about *esse* as about *quidditas*. When he said in the *De Ente
et Essentia* that I could understand what a phoenix was he
must have meant that I can know what the word 'phoenix'
means; since there are no phoenixes, I cannot have con-
ducted a scientific, physiological examination of the nature
of phoenixes. Later he is careful to distinguish between two
sorts of understanding — two ways in which, for instance, I
might understand what salt is. I may simply possess the
concept salt in the sense of knowing what the word 'salt'
means. Or I may be able to give a scientific definition of salt
from which its properties may be deduced; as when a
chemist tells me that salt is sodium chloride. It is clearly
possible to know what a thing is in the first of these senses
without knowing what it is in the second; I can know what a
word means without being able to give a scientific account
of what the that word signifies. Aquinas often says that
before you can ask whether a thing exists (*an sit*) you have
to know what the word for it means — e.g. before inquiring
whether there is such a thing as a vacuum or not you have
to start from the meaning of the word 'vacuum' (*In Physic*
IV, 10, 507). But before you begin to investigate what a
thing is — what is its nature or essence — he says, you have
to know that it is (Ia, 22 ad 2). With hindsight, we can see
he was wrong here: you might know the essential properties
of an element from its place in the periodic table before you
know whether such an element is to be found in the world
or not. But at least the distinction between the *significatio*

nominis, which must be known before the *an sit?* can be asked, and the *quidditas,* which cannot be known until after answering the *an sit,* marks a sophistication and improvement by comparison with the passage about the phoenix in the *De Ente.*

Applying this new theory to God, Aquinas says that before the proofs of God's existence we know what the word 'God' means — the Five Ways depend on five different accounts of its meaning, e.g. first unmoved mover — but *what* God is we do not know ever in this life even after the proofs have convinced (Ia 3, 4 ad 2). We do know, however, according to Aquinas, and can prove philosophically, that what God is is identical with his *esse* (Ia, 3, 4 ad 2). Now what does *esse* mean here?

To answer this we must turn our attention to sentences containing '*est*' which begin with a word for a complete concrete substance — whether this word be a proper name such as 'Socrates' (e.g. IIIa 17, 2; *Quodl.* 9, 3) or a concept-term such as 'god' (*De Pot.* VII, 2, 11). Such sentences may continue in three different ways. (1) the word '*est*' may be followed by a predicate term which belongs in the first of Aristotle's categories, that of substance; as in the sentence '*Socrates est homo*'. (2) it may be followed by a predicate which belongs in one of the nine other Aristotelian categories; e.g. '*Socrates est albus*'. (3) It may be followed by a period, '*Socrates est*'.[1]

The first two cases are distinguished by Aquinas in a crucial passage already discussed (*Quodlibet* IX, 3). '*Esse*', he says, 'is strictly and truly attributed only to a self-subsistent thing; and to such a thing two kinds of *esse* are attributed. The first *esse* results from the things which make it a unified whole, and this is the unique substantial *esse* of the individual. The second *esse* is something added to the things which constitute it; this is an added or accidental *esse*:

---

[1] Even a sentence not containing '*est*' at all may signify *esse* since a predicate such as '*currit*' in '*Socrates currit*' can be replaced by '*est currens*' (In *Meta,* V, IX, 893).

as *being white* is attributed to Socrates when it is said "Socrates is white"'.[1]

The third case, in which '*est*' is followed by a period, is reducible, Aquinas explains, to the first, the *esse substantiale*. 'A thing is said to be in a certain manner according to each form which it has. If the form is constitutive of its essence, then in having that form a thing is said to be *simpliciter*.'[2] The *esse simpliciter* of Socrates is the *esse* which makes him Socrates. 'If any form or nature does not pertain to the personal *esse* of a subsistent individual, that *esse* is not called the *esse* of that person without qualification: as *being white* is an *esse* of Socrates not qua Socrates but qua white.'[3]

We may ask what is the relationship between this *esse accidentale* which Socrates has when he is white, and the accidental form which the predicate of 'Socrates is white' is said to stand for. Is Socrates' being white one and the same thing as the whiteness of Socrates? Similarly, is Socrates' being human the same thing as the humanity of Socrates? Sometimes Aquinas, as one would expect, treats the members of these pairs as indistinguishable;[4] but in places he draws a distinction between them in terms of actuality and potentiality. Goodness and humanity, he says, are not signified in actuality save insofar as we signify that they

[1] Esse ergo proprie et vere non attribuitur nisi rei per se subsistenti; huic autem attribuitur esse duplex. Unum scilicet esse resultans ex his quibus eius unitas integratur, quod proprium est esse suppositi substantiale. Aliud est supposito attributum praeter ea quae integrant ipsum; quod est esse superadditum, scilicet accidentale; ut esse album attributur Socrati cum dicitur, Socrates est albus.

[2] Secundum quamlibet formam habitam, habens aliqualiter esse dicatur. Si ergo forma illa non sit praeter essentiam habentis sed constituat eius essentiam, ex eo quod habet talem formam, dicitur habens ease simpliciter.

[3] Si aliqua forma vel natura est quae non pertineat ad esse personale hypostasis subsistentis, illud esse non dicitur esse illius personae simpliciter, sed secundum quid: sicut esse album est esse Socratis, non inquantum est Socrates, sed inquantum est albus. IIIa, 17, 2c.

[4] e.g. *De Pot.* VII, 2; *In III Sent* d. 6. q. 2. a. 2.

are.[1] Only if John *is* good, not just if he will be, or can be, or is thought to be good, will John's goodness be actual and not merely potential. So the *esse album* of Socrates appears to be not simply the form, Socrates' whiteness, but the actual having of the form; but of course that form will itself only have real existence, or *esse*, if Socrates has *esse album*. It is in this sense that Aquinas says that *esse* is the actuality of every form and nature.[2]

But though form and *esse* are not identical, in so far as *esse* is the actuality of a form, it is clear that there cannot be *esse* without form. This is something which Aquinas often repeats: *omnis res habet esse per formam*; to be is to be F, where 'F' keeps a place for something which stands for a form. When the being in question is substantial being — *esse simpliciter*, denoted by *est* with a period — then the expression which takes the place of F must be an expression for the essence of the substance in question. The essence of Socrates is his humanity; so for Socrates to be is for him to be a human being. 'Socrates is' is equivalent to 'Socrates is a human being' if this second sentence is not taken to be a merely classificatory sentence (which would apply to a dead Socrates whose humanity was not actual) but as meaning that Socrates is actually a being capable of performing the operations characteristic of human nature. Let us write 'IS' rather than 'is' when the word is to be understood in this sense. Then 'Socrates IS' will be equivalent to 'Socrates is alive'. As Aquinas frequently said, echoing Aristotle, for living beings, to be is to be alive.[3] Other things are in being in different ways: for instance, ice is in being in a pond when

---

[1] Ia 3, 4c.   [2] Ia 3, 4c.

[3] *De An* 415b 13; *In I Sent* d 33 q 1 a 1; Ia 182 sed c. At IIIa 17 2c we are told that being a man, with all that is essential to this (having head, body, soul etc.) constitutes the *esse personale* of Socrates: In Socrate ponitur aliud esse secundum quod est albus, aliud secundum quod est homo: quia esse album non pertinet ad ipsum esse personale Socratis. Esse autem capitatum, et esse corporeum, et ease animatum, totum pertinet ad unam personam Socratis; et ideo ex omnibus his non fit nisi unum esse in Socrate.

what is in the pond solidifies.[1] Consequently, if we are to know what we mean when we say 'X est' we have to be able to supply the appropriate complement 'F' to refer to the essence or nature of X.[2] Now what of God's being? On the account we have just sketched to say that God IS, is to say that he is living a divine life; he is a living F, where F is the predicate defining what it is for the essence of God to function.

Now what is this predicate? In what does divine life consist? Sometimes, Aquinas says that we do not know: God's essence eludes us (Ia, 2,2, ad 2). This seems at first sensible modesty; but it is less modest than it appears; because Aquinas has such high standards of what knowledge is that it turns out that the essences of at most few things are known to us.[3] Moreover, Aquinas is prepared to tell us what the predicate is which replaces F when we rephrase 'God IS', as 'God IS F'. It is 'esse'. For this is the meaning of Aquinas' best known doctrine about God, namely that God's essence is *esse*, or that in God essence and *esse* are identical. (From *De Ente* to Ia 3, 4.)

If we are to make anything of this at all, it is clear that the sense of 'esse' here must be something different from that we have just elaborated, in which '. . . est' is to be expanded into 'IS F'; otherwise we shall set off in an unending stutter 'est, est, est . . .'. And there are a number of passages in Aquinas which make clear what this sense is supposed to be.

[1] *In VIII Meta* 11, 1694, following Aristotle H 1042b 25; cf. Owen, 76ff.

[2] If two substantial predicates can be true of the same individual (as Aquinas believed was the case when the Son of God became man in Christ) this does not involve two substantial *esses* (III1 17, 2); but in every case an enduring *esse* involves an enduring essence.

[3] Cf. ScG IV, I; 'Formae substantiales, quae secundum se sunt nobis ignotae, innotescunt per accidentalia'. This passage, and some others (Ia 29, 1 ad 3; Ia 77 1 ad 7; *De Ver.* 4, 1 ad 8 and 10, 1c) suggest that almost all essences are unknown. Other texts are less agnostic (Ia, 13, 8 ad 2; IIIa, 25, 5 ad 4).

Several times Aquinas speaks of 'esse' as being a very general, very fundamental predicate which is part of the nature of everything, and which is related to generic predicates (such as '. . . is an animal') in the way that such a generic predicate is related to a specific predicate (such as '. . . is a dog'). Thus, at *In V Met* 596 he speaks of a substantial *esse* 'which everything has in its nature'. At Ia, 65, 3 he says 'That which underlies is always found to be commoner than that which informs and restricts; as being is commoner than living, and living than thinking'.[1] Here it is clear what 'commoner' means: just as whatever thinks is alive, but not vice versa, so whatever is alive is being, but not vice versa. 'Underlying' seems to mean: to be a determinable which can be further determined; 'to be alive' being taken to be a particularization, determination, of 'to be'; perhaps in the way that 'to be red' is a determination of 'to be coloured' and 'to be chaste but not yet' is a restriction of 'to be chaste'. The clearest statement of this account of *esse* comes in a proof of God's existence which Aquinas offers in *De Pot* VIIc. There he says: Wherever causes whose proper effects are diverse produce also a common effect, the additional common effect must be produced in virtue of some superior cause of which it is the proper effect. For example, pepper and ginger, besides producing their own proper effects have it in common that they produce heat; they do this in virtue of the causality of fire, of which heat is the proper effect. Now all created causes have their own proper effects, but they also have a single common effect which is being (*esse*). Heat causes things *to be* hot, and builders cause there *to be* houses; both alike, therefore, cause being. There must, therefore, be some superior cause whose proper effect is being: and this, we are left to conclude, is what men call God.[2]

[1] Semper autem id quod substernitur in rebus, invenitur communius quam id quod informat et restringit ipsum: sicut esse quam vivere et vivere quam intelligere.

[2] Ad cuius evidentiam considerandum est, quod cum aliquae causae effectus diversos producentes communicant in uno effectu, praeter

Clearly, *being* in this argument is a common attribute which is possessed automatically by anything which possesses any substantial or accidental form. (It does not seem to be merely a disjunctive attribute; such that, to have being is either to be hot or to be a house . . . etc.; otherwise it would be absurd to ask for a cause of being in addition to a cause of being hot, and being a house). 'To be', so understood, seems to be the thinnest possible kind of predicate; to be, so understood, is to have that attribute which is common to mice and men, dust and angels. This attribute, being common to every substance, could hardly constitute the particular essence of any subject.

There are many passages where Aquinas seems to deny that *esse* is a more uninformative predicate than the more specific ones, where he seems to claim that it is in some way richer in content. For instance, at Ia, 3, 1 ad 3, on God's perfection, he puts the objection '*Esse* seems to be the most imperfect thing; since it is commonest, and altogether determinable (*recipiens omnium additiones*)'. His answer is: '*esse* is the most perfect of all things: it is more actual than

---

diversos effectus oportet quod illud commune producant ex virtute aliquius superioris causae cuius illud est proprius effectus. Et hoc ideo, quia cum proprius effectus producatur ab aliqua causa secundum suam propriam naturam vel formam, diversae causae habentes diversas naturas et formas oportet quod habeant proprios effectus diversos. Unde si in aliquo uno effectu conveniunt, ille non est proprius alicuius earum, sed alicuius superioris, in cuius virtute agunt; sicut patet quod diversa complexionata conveniunt in calefaciendo, ut piper, et zinziber, et similia, quamvis unumquodque eorum habeat suum proprium effectum diversum ab effectu alterius. Unde effectum communem oportet reducere in priorem causam cuius sit proprius, scilicet in ignem . . . Omnes autem causae creatae communicant in uno effectu qui est esse, licet singulae proprios effectus habeant, in quibus distinguuntur. Calor enim facit calidum esse, et aedificator facit domum esse. Conveniunt ergo in hoc quod causant esse: differunt autem in hoc quod ignis causat ignem, et aedificator causat domum. Oportet ergo esse aliquam causam superiorem omnibus cuius virtute omnia causent esse, et cuius esse sit proprius effectus (De Pot 7, 2c).

anything else; since nothing has actuality, except in so far as it is; and so *esse* is the actuality of all things and even of all forms.' But this answer makes use of the sense of *esse* in which it means 'actually being F' and calls for a paraphrase; whereas the objection depended on the sense of *esse* in which it is a predicate common to all substances—it is *this* predicate which is 'imperfect'.

If we are to be guided by the *De Potentia* passage, it is something very like this predicate— this very thin and uninformative predicate— which Aquinas thinks is the substitution for F in 'God IS F'. I say 'it is something very like', because there are several criticisms which any scholastic would make of the suggestion that God's existence just *was* his possession of this predicate. The very first objection which Aquinas makes to his proposal to identify God's essence with God's *esse* is this. 'If this were so, then God's *esse* would have nothing added to it. But the *esse* to which no addition is made, is the common *esse* which is predicated of all things; and so it would follow that God is the being predicable of everything. But this is false, according to the Book of Wisdom 14, 21: they gave the incommunicable name to stocks and stones. So God's *esse* is not his essence.' It is clear, I think, that the *ens commune* is the predicate I have explicated, which really does belong to stocks and stones. When Aquinas speaks of God's *esse* 'having nothing added to it' he means that if God's *esse* is his existence, then we must say not that God is such-and-such a kind of thing, but that God is, period. His answer to the difficulty goes thus: 'To which no addition is made' can be understood in two ways. In one way, it is a part of the meaning of the term that something should not be added to it: as it is part of the meaning of 'irrational animal' that it should be without reason. In another way, 'to which no addition is made' means that it is not part of its meaning that something should be added to it: as the common term 'animal' is without reason in the sense that it is not part of the meaning of this common term that it should have reason; but neither is it part of its meaning that it should lack reason. *Esse* without addition,

in the first sense, is the divine *esse*; *esse* without addition in
the second sense, is the common *esse*.[1]

Here Aquinas, in order to prevent God's *esse* from being
the applicability of a quite uninformative predicate, turns
it into the applicability of a predicate which is no predicate
at all. What he says comes to this. When we say, of anything
but God, that it IS, we mean that for some F, (to be specified
in the particular case) it IS F; when we say of God that he IS,
we mean the same except that no predicate may be sub-
stituted for the F which occurs in the formula. God isn't
anything of any kind, he just is. But this is surely complete
nonsense. For the only meaning that attaches to a formula
such as

> God IS F

is that if you substitute a genuine predicate for the dummy
letter F, you will get a meaningful sentence. If you forbid
such a substitution, you must delete the variable letter
(which is as it were a permission to make a substitution), and
you are left simply with 'God is . . .' which — if the dots are
not a variable, as they must not be — is just an incomplete
sentence. So interpreted, the incommunicable name seems
to be just an ill-formed formula.

But the absurdity does not stop there. God, for Aquinas,
is not just pure *ens*, period; he is *ipsum esse subsistens*; that is
to say, the predicate is applied to God not in its concrete, but
in its abstract form. God does not just be, he is being. This
to be understood on the model of 'the idea of heat is not just
hot, it is heat'. The Platonic parallel is drawn by Aquinas
himself. In order to prove that God has no accidents, he

---

[1] Aliquid cui non fit additio potest intelligi dupliciter. Uno modo
ut de ratione ejus sit quod non fiat ei additio, sicut de ratione animalis
irrationalis est quod sit sine ratione. Alio modo intelligitur aliquid cui
non fit additio quia non est de ratione ejus quod sibi fiat additio, sicut
animal commune est sine ratione, quia non est de ratione animalis
communis ut habeat rationem, sed nec de ratione ejus est ut careat
ratione. Primo igitur modo esse sine additione est esse divinum,
secundo modo esse since additione est esse commune.

appeals to the fact that God is his *esse*, and quotes Boethius 'being itself can have nothing else added to it'. 'Just so, he says, what is hot can have extra things besides being hot, e.g. whiteness; but heat itself has nothing except heat' (Ia 3, 6c). What all men call 'God', on this account, is the Platonic idea of Being.

The objections, therefore, which have been made during the centuries to Plato's theory of Ideas apply to Aquinas' theory of God as subsistent being. But this is not all that is wrong with the theory: for the predicate to which the Platonic extrapolation is applied is, as we have seen, a very extraordinary predicate. Either it is understood as a predicate which holds of all substances; in which case it is too uninformative to constitute the essence of any entity; or it is understood as a variable expression which permits of no substitution, in which case it is an ill-formed formula. The notion of *Ipsum Esse Subsistens*, therefore, so far from being a profound metaphysical analysis of the divine nature, turns out to be the Platonic Idea of a predicate which is at best uninformative and at worst unintelligible.

6

The Fifth Way

The Fifth way is based on the directedness of things. We observe that some things which lack awareness, namely natural bodies, act for the sake of an end. This is clear because they always or commonly act in the same manner to achieve what is best, which shows that they reach their goal not by chance but because they tend towards it. Now things which lack awareness do not tend towards a goal unless directed by something with awareness and intelligence, like an arrow by an archer. Therefore there is some intelligent being by whom everything in nature is directed to a goal, and this we call 'God.'[1]

The fifth way has an obvious similarity to the popular Argument from Design, but two differences should be noted at the outset. First, Aquinas is not here arguing from such phenomena as the instinctive behaviour of animals. His starting point is the end-directedness of things which lack

[1] Quinta via sumitur ex gubernatione rerum. Videmus enim quod aliqua quae cognitione carent, scilicet corpora naturalia, operantur propter finem, quod apparet ex hoc quod semper aut frequentius eodem modo operantur et consequuntur id quod est optimum, unde patet quod non a casu sed ex intentione perveniunt ad finem. Ea autem quae non habent cognitionem non tendunt in finem nisi directa ab aliquo cognoscente et intelligente, sicut sagitta a sagittatore. Ergo est aliquis intelligens a quo omnes res naturales ordinantur ad finem, et hoc dicimus Deum.

consciousness, which he calls 'natural bodies': he means the lifeless elements, and perhaps the plants and heavenly bodies. Secondly, it is not clear whether he is arguing that there are particular phenomena which exhibit a teleology which must originate in intelligence, or whether he is saying that the universe as a whole displays an order which must be the design of a designer. When he says that things act to achieve what is best, does he mean what is best for themselves, or does he mean some universal good, such as he mentions at Ia, 15, 2, where he says 'that which is best in things is the good of the order of the universe?' Probably he means that they act for their own good: certainly this is a more plausible claim than the claim that natural bodies act for the good of the universe. But if we understand the premise in this way, we meet a difficulty and a parallel ambiguity in the conclusion, 'there is some intelligent being by whom everything in nature is directed *ad finem*'. Does '*ad finem*' mean 'to its goal' or 'to a single goal'? And if the former, by analogy with the premise, does he mean that for each natural thing there is an intelligence (perhaps a different one from case to case) which directs it to its goals, or that there is a single intelligence which directs every natural thing to its goal? The second alternative is the only natural reading of the Latin, and the only one which could license the clause 'and this we call "God" '; yet the former alternative seems to be all that follows from the premise. Once again, we seem to meet the familiar quantifier shift:

(1) Every unconscious teleological agent is directed by some intelligence
(2) There is some intelligence which directs every unconscious teleological agent.[1]

Elsewhere, Aquinas says things which bring the Fifth

[1] Writing 'Ux' for 'x is unconscious', 'Tx' for 'x is teleological agent', 'Ix' for 'x is intelligent', 'Dxy' for 'x directs y', we have

(1) $\forall x(Ux \& Tx \rightarrow \exists y(Iy \& Dyx))$
(2) $\exists y(Iy \& \forall x(Ux \& Tx \rightarrow Dyx))$

Way nearer to the traditional argument from design. He produces more familiar examples of teleology in nature, many of them borrowed from Aristotle. The leaves in plants are arranged to protect the fruit; the foot is made by nature apt for walking; front teeth are good for biting, back teeth are good for chewing (ScG III, 3; *In Physics* II, 12 252). As examples of instinctive activities of brutes, he mentions the swallow's building of its nest and the spider's weaving of its web (*In Physics* II, 13 259).

Elsewhere, also, he offers *a priori* proofs that any agent, even unconscious, must act for an end. The fullest set of such proofs comes in the second chapter of book three of the *Summa contra Gentiles*. Aquinas begins by defining an end (*finis*) as 'that towards which the drive (*impetus*) of an agent tends', whether or not the agent succeeds in reaching it: he gives as examples a doctor working to cure, a runner running towards a winning post, a target which is the end of the motion of an arrow. 'Now the drive of every agent' he goes on, 'is towards something definite; it is not the case that just any action issues from just any power; but heating issues from heat, and cooling from coldness'.[1] Some actions, like building and healing, terminate in a product (a house, the health of the patient); others, like understanding and sensation, do not. In the former case, 'the drive of the agent terminates through the action in the product', in the second 'the drive of the agent tends towards the action itself'. In either case — in all cases, in fact — the agent in acting tends towards (*intendat*) an end.

The second argument is rather complicated, but its essentials are as follows. A final end is one after whose achievement an agent stops striving (*non conatur ulterius*). Now the action of an agent cannot go on for ever. So there must be something after whose achievement the agent's strivings end; so every agent acts for an end.

---

[1] Omnis autem agentis impetus ad aliquid certum tendit: non enim ex quacunque virtute quaevis actio procedit, sed a calore quidem calefactio, a frigore autem infrigidatio.

The third argument begins by dividing agents into two classes: natural agents (*agentia per naturam*) and intelligent agents (*agentia per intellectum*).[1] Intelligent agents conceive beforehand in their minds what they are to achieve by action, and act upon this preconception. 'And just as in the intellect conceiving beforehand there exists a complete likeness of the effect which is to be achieved by the actions of the intelligent agent, so also a likeness of a natural effect pre-exists in the agent, which is what determines the action to the effect in question: for fire produces fire, and an olive produces another olive.'[2]

The fourth argument is an Aristotelian one. There can only be faults (*peccata*) where things are directed to certain ends: it is no fault in a grammarian to be unable to heal, but it is in a doctor. But there are faults in nature, no less than in the operations of skill: for instance, monstrous births. So there are natural agents which act for ends.

In the next chapter Aquinas seeks to show that every agent acts for the sake of some *good*. Most of his arguments cover the same ground; the most important new one runs as follows. If something happens as the result of an agent's action without being aimed at, then it happens by chance or luck. But almost always in the workings of nature we find the best happening. If this happened without being aimed at by the natural agent (*praeter intentionem naturalis agentis*) it would be by chance or luck. But this is impossible, because things which happen always or commonly are not chance or fortuitous events. So natural agents aim at what is best (*id quod melius est*).

So, in effect, we have five arguments to show that every agent acts for an end: one from the determinacy of action, one from the impossibility of acting for ever, one from the

[1] This translation is not strictly accurate, for a man digesting his food is an intelligent agent, but acts *per naturam*, not *per intellectum*.

[2] Sicut autem in intellectu praeconcipiente existit tota similitudo effectus ad quem per actiones intelligentis pervenitur, ita in agente naturali praeexistit similitudo naturalis effectus, ex qua actio ad hunc effectum determinatur: nam ignis generat ignem, et oliva olivam.

likeness between cause and effect, one from faults in nature, and one from the non-fortuitous production of good.

None of these arguments is sound, but an examination of them casts light on Aquinas' notion of teleology. We must notice first that when Aquinas attributes ends or aims (*intentiones*) to inanimate objects, he is not being crudely anthropomorphic. He is not attributing to stocks and stones ghostly half-conscious purposes. He insists, and indeed makes it a major step in his argument, that inanimate objects have no consciousness (*cognitio*), and if he speaks of their natural desires (e.g. *in III Sent* d1, q. 1, a 4) he means simply, what he more often says, their natural tendencies (*appetitus*). We must remember secondly that when Aquinas speaks of natural agents and their actions, he does not mean just any behaviour of bodies; the paradigm he has in mind is hot bodies heating, cold bodies cooling, wet bodies wetting and dry bodies drying.

This is clear in the first argument from the determinacy of natural effects. The hot does not cool, Aquinas says, and the cold does not heat, but particular powers have particular effects. In so far as it is true at all, it seems to be a logical truth that only what is wet wets; a linguistic philosopher might say that it was a grammatical remark drawing attention to the connection between the adjective and the verb. So it seems that we will not need God to account for this wondrous adaptation of agents to their operations. However, it is not difficult to replace Aquinas' remark with a less vacuous example. Water, when cooled, turns into ice and not into, say, coal. But what has this to do with goals? Explain, if you like, the freezing of water by saying that water has a natural tendency to freeze; but why say that water is aiming at anything in freezing? Aquinas' argument suggests that what is being aimed at is the freezing itself; but this amounts to saying that water freezes because it freezes. It is true that we sometimes explain the actions of human agents by saying they were performed for their own sake, as ends in themselves. But this differs from the case of the natural agents in two ways. First of all, the actions are voluntary ones; whereas the actions of natural bodies are necessitated by their nature. Second, to explain a human action in this way is to say that the agent did it because he *wanted to*; and his wanting can be identified in other ways than by appealing to his performance of the action when not impeded. Whereas in the case of the natural agent there is no wanting, but only a tendency. In the case of natural agents, 'A φd as an end in itself' collapses into 'A φd because A has a natural tendency to φ' as it does not in the case of intellectual agents.

So much for the case where the act is an end in itself. Aquinas claims another type of natural teleology when actions have a product. Very many verbs describing the actions of animate and inanimate agents describe them in terms of the state of affairs which they bring about, which is their result, the state of affairs which obtains after the action has been performed, e.g. to open the door is to bring it about that the door is open, to kill someone is to bring it about that he is dead. Aquinas' paradigm actions might well be thought to fall into this class: to heat things is to bring it about that they are hot, to wet things is to bring it about that they are wet. All such verbs describe actions in terms of their end states: thus, in the scholastic tag, 'actions are specified by their ends' (IIa, I, 1, 3). (You can dry things in many different ways, e.g. by wiping them or blowing hot air on them: it is the identity of the result that makes the different activities both cases of drying.) There are other verbs which describe processes in terms of their beginning-states: e.g. 'fall off', 'run away from'. There are others which describe processes without reference to either—e.g., 'wipe', 'run', 'fall', 'move'. Aquinas' argument seems to depend on the existence of the first class of verbs and to involve a confusion between

(3) Some things have a natural tendency to perform actions specified by certain ends

and (4) Some things have a tendency to perform actions for the sake of certain ends.

Aquinas' second argument from the impossibility of acting for ever, is open to the following objection. For E to be
the end or purpose of behaviour B it is neither necessary nor
sufficient that the agent should rest after achieving E. It is
not necessary because the agent may at once go on to aim at
something else; it is not sufficient because the agent may
cease to act simply because it is tired. The fact that animals
sleep does not make whatever happens before they go to
sleep the aim or purpose of their previous activity. Of course
it is true that once an agent has achieved an end, his further
activity is no longer aimed at that end, and in that sense 'his
strivings cease'. But in order to know which bits of his
behaviour are strivings one already has to know what his
ends are; and one cannot deduce this simply from his strivings. Aquinas argues that since an endless series of actions
cannot be completed, an endless series of actions cannot be
aimed at, since nothing can aim at what is impossible; so an
agent could not even start on an endless series of actions.
Since the agent cannot be aiming at an endless series, he
argues, it must be aiming at a series with an end. But of
course what needed proving was that agents must be said
to 'aim' at all; and the question is begged when we are
asked: is the series of actions the agent is aiming at finite
or endless?

Aquinas' third argument is based on the principle that
like causes like. Waiving difficulties about the sense and
validity of this principle, we can still ask how it shows that
like acts *in order to* bring about its like? Because, Aquinas
says, the agent's tendency is to a particular result determined by its nature: fire sets on fire, olives beget olives. But
in that case this argument collapses into the first argument,
from determinacy of action.

Unlike the earlier three arguments the Aristotelean
argument from faults in nature seems a valid one: to regard
something as a deficient specimen of a species, or to regard
a natural process as having misfired, certainly is to look at
nature with a teleological eye. But the conclusion of this
argument is much less sweeping than the one Aquinas

draws from it. It simply proves that there are some natural phenomena which can be described teleologically, not that every natural agent acts for an end.

Aquinas' final argument was based on the dichotomy: either end-directed or chance. This dichotomy is similar to one used by those modern philosophers who have argued that freewill presupposes determinism and is inconceivable without it. For instance, A. J. Ayer wrote that responsibility presupposes determinism because 'if it is a matter of pure chance that a man should act in one way rather than another he may be free but he can hardly be responsible'(Ayer, 275). Both Aquinas and Ayer seem to be reducing a trichotomy to a dichotomy. There are three possibilities: that an action is caused *ex ante* by natural tendencies; that it is to be explained *ex post* by teleological factors; and that it is a matter of chance. Ayer argues that the actions of responsible agents cannot be a matter of (3), therefore they must be a matter of (1). Aquinas argues that the actions of natural agents cannot be a case of (3), therefore they must be a case of (2). What each of them needs to show, but fails to show, is that (1) and (2) are coextensive — either, in Ayer's sense, that all apparently teleological explanations are reducible to mechanistic explanations; or in Aquinas' sense, that all apparently mechanistic explanations involve a teleological element. But it is the relationship between (1) and (2) that is our real concern and this is not illuminated by pointing out the difference between (1) and (2) on the one hand and (3) on the other.

Each of Aquinas' arguments, then, breaks down in its attempt to prove that every agent acts for the sake of an end; and without this *a priori* principle one may well be sceptical whether natural, non-living agents act for ends. However, the more modest statement of the Fifth Way, that some things which lack consciousness act for the sake of an end, seems acceptable as a premise if supported by the other examples drawn from the behaviour of living organisms. The interesting philosophical question is whether the teleological explanation of animal behaviour is irreducible to any non-teleological explanation.

The whole idea of teleological explanation has been for long suspect in philosophical and scientific circles. It was recently reintroduced as a topic for philosophical discussion by Charles Taylor in his book *The Explanation of Behaviour* (1964). Taylor argues that the question whether there are irreducibly teleological phenomena in nature is an empirical one, which cannot be settled either in the negative or in the affirmative by *a priori* philosophical reasonings. It cannot be settled in the negative, he contended, because the negative argument against teleology is based on the premise that teleological laws make behaviour a function of the state of some unobservable entity, a purpose or a power like a *virtus dormitive* whose operation cannot be predicted *ex ante* and which is itself indetectable apart from the behaviour to which it gives rise. But this premise, he says, is mistaken. An explanation of a certain behaviour B might simply be that the state of a system S and its environment E was such that B was required to achieve an end G by which the system's purpose was defined. In such a case S, E, B, G and the law correlating them might all be empirically observable. Moreover, the teleological law in question might be irreplaceable by any non-teleological law; for though any antecedent condition of S and E which requires B for G will also fulfil a non-teleological description "SE" this does not mean that B is a function of SE, for in other cases SE may occur without B occurring, precisely in the case in which SE is not also a case of requiring B for G. On the other hand, Taylor argued, the issue could not be settled *a priori* in favour of teleology. He did not cite the *a priori* Aristotelean arguments we have been considering, but considered certain arguments of ordinary language philosophers. It has been pointed out, Taylor says, that everyday accounts of behaviour, in terms of action and desire, are teleological explanations which carry the implication that no non-teleological account is valid. But it does not follow from the fact that we can use these teleological concepts in our description of human behaviour that a non-teleological account is impossible. We can all understand, Taylor says, the Aristotelean distinction between violent and natural motion, and we can sort out movements into these two categories just as we can distinguish in human life between action and non-action. But this does not mean that we can accept the criteria on which the Aristotelean distinction was putatively made. *A pari*, the everyday usefulness of the concepts of action and desire does not rule out the possibility of non-teleological explanation of human behaviour. To say that we may one day discover that our behaviour may be accounted for by a mechanistic theory is not to say that we may one day find we have been talking nonsense all our lives.

Denis Noble has questioned Taylor's defence of teleology against mechanist criticism (Noble (1)). He argues that if it is to be an empirically ascertainable matter whether a situation of a system and environment requires B for G, then there must be a non-teleological description applicable to all such situations, namely, one in terms of the empirical evidence used to ascertain that the situation verifies the teleological description. There could not be a case such as Taylor seemed to envisage, where a teleological explanation could be given of the phenomena without it being possible to give a non-teleological account. Therefore there cannot be teleological explanations which are basic and irreducible.

In reply, Taylor agreed with Noble that there could not be a case where two situations had exactly the same intrinsic description, and yet each required different behaviour to encompass the same goal. Yet in certain cases the teleological explanation may be basic for all that. Suppose we have case where in $(SE)_1$ it is the case that B_1 is required for G: let us express this by saying that in $(SE)_1$ the situation is characterized by the teleological antecedent T_1; (requiring B_1 for G_1). Suppose also that in SE_2, B_2 is required for G, i.e. T_2 holds. The teleological and non-teleological accounts are not necessarily here on a level.

'Suppose it be the case that the set of correlations $(SE)_1 - B_1$, $(SE)_2 - B_2$ . . . $(SE)_n - B_n$ exhibit no intrinsic order, so that they leave us just as incapable of predicting what will happen in situation $(SE)_n + 1$ as we would have been before establishing this set of correlations; suppose in other words it be the case that these correlations are not instances of a general non-teleological law $B = f(SE)$, then we would clearly have a teleological account without a corresponding non-teleological one. For the correlations $T_1 - B_1 \ldots T_n - B_n$ do permit extrapolation to new cases: we know for each new situation that B will occur which is required by this situation if G is to come about. We have only to examine situation $n + 1$ to see what it requires for G and we can predict what B will be like in this situation. . . . The correlations of the $(SE)_x - B_x$ form, on this hypothesis, form a disparate set which can be predicted and explained by the law $B = f(T)$. This latter, then, provides a more basic level of explanation' (Taylor (2) 142).

In reply, Noble said that 'the question whether the $(SE)_n - B_n$ correlations exhibit an order which may be used in formulating a non-teleological explanation (i.e. a theory which allows us to predict the $n + 1$th case) is not primarily an empirical matter . . . except in the rather trivial sense that it is an empirical matter whether or not the theoretician has yet discovered such an order. . . . For, if the correlations are regular at all they must exhibit *an* order, and the question, what sorts of order count as explanation, is a conceptual, not an empirical investigation' (Noble (2), 63). At this point, the disagreement between Taylor and Noble begins to appear rather marginal, since in his original book Taylor, when saying that the question whether animate organisms were purposive was an empirical question, wrote 'The word "empirical" here may mislead. In fact what is at stake here is not an ordinary matter of fact, such as whether rabbits eat lettuce; it concerns the form of the laws to be used in explanation and the concepts in which these laws are to be cast' (Taylor (1), 100). Taylor calls the question empirical because it concerns the forms and concepts of laws relating *empirical* phenomena; Noble calls the question conceptual because it concerns the forms and *concepts* of those laws.

Some disagreement remains, however. The two authors appear to be using the expression "basic explanation" in a different sense: Taylor regards an explanation of the behaviour of a system as being more basic the more behaviour of that system that it explains; Noble regards an explanation as being more basic the more systems it can explain the behaviour of. To bring this out, consider the behaviour of a simple thermostat. (I choose an artefact as an example for simplicity's sake; the crucial philosophical problems are the same whether we consider artificial or natural teleological systems.) Let us suppose it operates to maintain a temperature of 60°. In supposing this, of course, we are casting our description of its behaviour in teleological form: it does whatever is required to achieve the goal of the temperature's being 60°. As Noble's original argument shows, however, we shall always be able to replace any teleological description of the state of the system and its environment (e.g. requiring an increase of temperature of 5° to reach a temperature of 60°) with a non-teleological description of the same situation (being at a temperature of 55°). Taylor is surely right in saying that, in such a case, the teleological formula will be both more useful in predicting, and more satisfactory in explaining the behaviour of the system. The Noble formula for converting teleological into non-teleological descriptions of the situation will yield in the first instance only a banal set of correlations (e.g., at 55° it increases the temperature by 5°; at 56° it increases the temperature by 4°) which need exhibit no order other than the order more compendiously exhibited by the teleological formula. To this extent, Taylor is right in calling the teleological explanation more basic.

However, we know that in this case the teleological explanation is reducible to a mechanistic one in a non-trivial manner also. The behaviour of the system can be explained in terms of the expansion of metals or the magnetic properties of solenoids or whatever natural properties are utilized in the particular switching mechanism adopted. Given the existence of the system, this explanation has a claim to be regarded as more basic than the teleological one. It must be at least as successful as the teleological one at predicting the behaviour of the system: for it is only the efficiency of the mechanism which makes the teleological correlations hold. Moreover, knowledge of the mechanistic properties may enable one to predict the breakdown of the system, which the teleological explanation will not. Again, the properties which figure in the mechanistic explanation of this particular system will be properties which will figure also in the explanation of many other different systems, teleological and non-teleological. In this sense, then, the mechanistic explanation will be the more basic one.

Notice, however, the qualification inserted above: 'given the existence of the system'. For if we ask not how thermostats operate, but why there are such thermostatic systems as immersion heaters and refrigerators, the explanation is once more teleological: it is because human beings want to keep water hot and beer cool. And an explanation of why a system exists might be regarded, from one point of view, as more basic than an explanation of how a system operates.

Of course, there may be—as there is not at present— another level of explanation at which the end-directed behaviour of the human beings who design and construct heaters and refrigerators is capable of reduction to a mechanistic one—not just in a trival manner like the Noble-type reduction of the description of the behaviour of the thermostat, but in an illuminating manner like the exhibition of the relay mechanism. And again, there may be an explanation— mechanistic or teleological—of the existence of such systems as human beings. But however long mechanistic and teleological explanations succeed each other in this way, they cannot just play pat-a-cake with one another. The mechanistic explanation of the operation of the thermostat will be more basic—in one sense—than the teleological explanation of its operation, and the teleological explanation of its existence will remain more basic—in another sense—than the mechanistic explanation of its operation.

For our purposes, the upshot of the controversy seems to be this. Noble's demonstration of the trivial reducibility of teleological to non-teleological explanations of operations of a system does not show that there must exist a non-trivial reduction of that explanation to a mechanistic level; still less does it show that there must be a non-teleological explanation of the existence of the system.

Moreover, it seems that Noble must admit that the question whether there are non-trivial reductions of teleological explanations of human and animal behaviour is empirical in a strong sense. For he is prepared to agree that there can be no peripheralist non-teleological explanation of animate action: i.e. no explanation which does not take account of the internal neurophysiological structure of the animal. But it is an empirical fact, not a conceptual truth, that cats and monkeys and we ourselves do not have sawdust within our skulls instead of brains. But if we did have sawdust, then on Noble's own admission, there would be no non-teleological explanation of our behaviour. Of course, it is not an empirical *question* whether animals have sawdust within their heads; we know for certain they don't; but we do so on inductive not *a priori* grounds. And it still is an empirical question whether — admitting for the sake of argument that there is no philosophical argument *against* there being a mechanistic explanation — the structure of the human brain has the type of complexity necessary to provide a mechanistic explanation of the complexity of human behaviour.

It is time to connect the contemporary controversy with Aquinas. Taylor's concept of teleology differs in several ways from that of the *contra Gentiles*. For Taylor, the essence of a teleological law is that it describes regularities of operation in terms of end product rather than of antecedent conditions. For Aquinas, a more important feature of teleological explanation is that the end state should be *good* for the system whose operation is to be explained: it must be conducive to the system's survival and performance of its characteristic activities. Considered merely as a fund of *ex post* explanations of motions, Newtonian physics is no less teleological than Aristotelian. For Newton defined gravity as a centripetal force; and a centripetal force is 'that by which bodies are drawn or impelled, or in any way tend, towards a point as to a centre'. What Newton explained by gravity, Aristotle had sought to explain by postulating 'natural places' to which heavy bodies tended by their heaviness and light bodies tended by their lightness. What made this a fundamentally teleological account was that the natural place for each body was supposed to be the place in which it was best for that body to be, the place in which it was most likely to survive as it was.

For Aquinas, then, *ex post* regularly is not sufficient to constitute teleological explanation: nor is it necessary. The behaviour of rational agents is end-directed behaviour *par excellence*; yet it is distinguished from the behaviour of natural agents precisely by its irregularity. In Aquinas' terminology, *agentia per intellectum*, unlike *agentia per naturam*, are not *ordinata ad unum*: their activity is not limited to a single pattern. Such indeterminism, for Aquinas, is quite compatible with teleological explanation; at times he even treats it as a necessary condition for explanation to be fully teleological (*De Pot.* 1.5).

Paradoxically, it does not even seem to be necessary that teleological explanation should invoke an end-state at all. In modern times it is customary to make a distinction, which Aquinas does not make, between intentions and motives. Intentions are forward-looking reasons for action and motives backward-looking reasons: in the picturesque phrase of the jurisprudent Austin 'the intention is the aim of the act of which the motive is the spring'. To assign an intention to an action is to explain it in terms of its hoped upshot; but an explanation in terms of motive (e.g. 'out of envy' or 'because he helped me in the past') may give a reason for action in terms of a previous rather than a subsequent state of affairs. Similar considerations apply to the behaviour of animals: a sheep fleeing from a wolf is not running *to* anywhere (Cf. Kenny, Ch. 4.)

There are, therefore, three distinct dichotomies we may make between types of explanation: *ex post* vs *ex ante*, regularity vs non-regularity, beneficial vs non-beneficial. The factors which serve as criteria for the three distinctions vary independently of each other in a way which is obscured if we simply distinguish between teleological and non-teleological explanations. This is shown by the following table of the various possible types of explanation, with instances of the phenomena they explain.

1. *Ex ante*	Regular	Non-beneficial	e.g. Newtonian inertia
2. *Ex post*	Regular	Non-beneficial	e.g. Newtonian gravity
3. *Ex ante*	Regular	Beneficial	e.g. instinctive avoidance behaviour
4. *Ex post*	Regular	Beneficial	e.g. nest-building
5. *Ex ante*	Non-regular	Beneficial	e.g. human motivated action
6. *Ex post*	Non-regular	Beneficial	e.g. human intentional action

It will be seen that all except the first of these types of explanation can be regarded, from one or other point of view, as 'teleological'. The three criteria for so regarding explanations are distinct; but of course they are not disconnected. One way in which we decide whether an *ex ante* or *ex post* type of law is the appropriate one to seek in explanation of a motion is by seeing whether the observable regularities are more easily describable in terms of their *terminus a quo* or their *terminus ad quem*. Another is to see whether the *terminus ad quem* of the motion is something beneficial to the system.

　If we say, as the table above implies, that teleological explanation of human action must be in terms of something beneficial, the word 'beneficial' cannot be taken in quite the sense introduced before of 'conducive to survival and activity'. It may be by catering for the wants, rather than for the needs, of the agent that the hoped-for results of human actions count as beneficial. The needs of an agent are in general discovered by inquiry into the nature and condition of the agent; the wants of an agent are in general ascertained through their expression in the agent's behaviour. This expression may be, in the case of humans, linguistic or non-linguistic and in the case of all agents it may or may not consist in behaviour leading to the satisfaction of the want in question. For unless wants were expressible by some means other than want-satisfying behaviour, they could never be in any empirical sense explanatory factors. The satisfaction of a need is always, truistically, beneficial to an agent; the satisfaction of a want need not be, whether benefit is considered in terms of long-term wants or of survival.

The fulfilment of needs and the satisfaction of wants may be regarded as two different types of goal which a system may have. A third type of goal is a purpose imposed on the system from outside such as the function for which a manufacturer designs an artefact. We may ask: in defining a system, must one make reference to its goal or goals? In the case of artificial teleological systems, the answer seems to be yes: one could not explain what a watch was without mentioning that it was for telling the time. But does the same hold of natural objects, and in particular of living beings? Noble says 'apart from cases in which we have access to the maker's specifications (e.g. the specification that a system is designed, by an engineer or by God, to achieve a particular goal), to say that an animal has a particular goal is to make a hypothesis about it based on observations of the animal's behaviour' (Noble (2), 63). This seems to need qualification. It may be a hypothesis that a particular dog is looking for a particular bone; but it seems to be not an empirical hypothesis, but part of the concept *dog*, that dogs in general pursue such things as food and drink and sex. *That* there are dogs, that the world contains beings answering to the concept, is of course an empirical truth, and one which might cease to be true after some cosmic catastrophe. There seems something inconceivable in the notion of a purely mechanistic animal — an animal, that is, whose behaviour was *prima facie* mechanistic and not teleological. But it does not seem to be part of the concept *dog* that no mechanistic explanation can ever be forthcoming at a deeper level of his goal-seeking behaviour. Even in the case of human beings, it seems to me that Taylor is wrong when he says that our everyday teleo-

logical account of behaviour in terms of action and desire
carries the implication that no non-teleological account is
valid. It is true that they imply that no non-teleological
account *purely in terms of the environment* is valid; and this is
the only conclusion which Taylor's detailed examples
support. But that is a different claim.

The fact that a system has a goal, then, does not prove
that it is not fundamentally mechanistic. But must a system
have a goal at all? It seems that there are systems which
operate to produce regular and periodic changes such that
it is impossible to single out any of the successive states of
the system as being its goal. The oxygen cycle seems to be
one such example,[1] and so, *pace* Aristotle and Aquinas, does
the alternation of the seasons and the solar system as a
whole.

In what way is a goalless system a system at all? In-
tuitively, I suppose, one would define a system as a group of
elements interacting with each other in such a way that the
history of any element is more easily predicted from the
history of the remaining elements than it is from the history
of comparable elements of the environment. A simple
example of this is the way in which the different parts of my
body move together with each other much more than they
move together with any chair, room, vehicle or other item
in my environment. The environment of a system must be
regarded as everything which is not part of the system. The
definition is, of course, both vague and circular; but there
is no harm in the circularity, and no remedy for the vague-
ness.

It is a consequence of this account of a system that the
existence of a system may call for an explanation distinct
from the explanation of its operation. This was a point
noticed earlier in the discussion of thermostats: the mechanistic explanation of the operation of a refrigerator does not
supersede the teleological explanation of its existence. It was

[1] I owe this example to Mr. A. Ross, formerly of Linacre College,
Oxford.

also a point made by Aquinas when discussing Empedocles as reported by Aristotle. Empedocles had argued
that one should not say that the rain rained in order to water
the crops, but should rather explain it in terms of the con-
densation of vapour in cold high altitudes. Otherwise one
might as well say it fell in order to destroy the crops, which
it sometimes does. Aquinas replied that the two explanations
were not incompatible. No doubt the rain fell because of the
mechanistic factors mentioned by Empedocles; this did not
prevent it being ordered to the preservation of mortals.[1]
The increase of the crops was indeed too particular a result
to assign as the general purpose of rain; none the less, the
beneficial effects of rain were more frequent than its dele-
terious effects, so there was no case for saying that it was for
the sake of destruction (*In Phys* II, 254).

Aquinas' example is ill-chosen, his general philosophical
point correct. In the case of living organisms at least we
know that there are mechanistic systems controlled by the
finalities of larger systems. But the further question remains:
should we look for a further explanation of the existence of
these finalistic systems, as we look for an explanation of the
refrigerator's existence? To this question, Aristotle answered
yes. To the same question Darwin later gave the answer of
Aquinas; but whereas the further explanation given by
Aquinas was itself a teleological one, in terms of a Creator's
purpose, the explanation sought by Darwin was a mechanistic one in terms of natural selection.[2]

---

[1] Nam pluvia licet habeat necessariam causam ex parte materiae,
tamen ordinatur ad finem aliquem, scilicet ad conservationem rereum
generabilium et corruptibilium.

[2] Aquinas was familiar with, and rejected, some of the principles
of natural selection, which were anticipated by Empedocles rather as
the principles of the atomic theory were ancitipated by Leucippus and
Democritus. Aquinas thus reports Empedocles: A principio con-
stitutionis mundi, quatuor elementa convenerunt ad constitutionem
rerum naturalium: et in quibuscumque omnia sic acciderunt apta ad
aliquam utilitatem, sicut si propter hoc facta essent, illa tantum
conservata sunt, eo quod habuerunt dispositionem apta ad conserva-

Each of these types of explanation raises further questions. Let us take the latter first. Let us assume that broadly Darwinian explanations can be found for the existence of the teleological organisms we see around us: does our investigation rest there? Or can the universe itself be regarded as a system which operates, through mechanistic means, to the goal of producing species of organisms, in the way that a refrigerator works through mechanistic means to the goal of a uniform temperature? Is the universe itself one huge machine, a goal-directed system?

This seems to be the appropriate contemporary version of the old argument from design. The medieval version of that argument depended to a great extent on antiquated astronomy. Austin Farrer has put it well.

'It is sometimes stated that the universe is a design or covered by a design; and as one system of action in me corresponds to the action of one intelligence, so the far vaster and more complex system of the world to the operation of a proportionate intelligence. But there is no empirical evidence for the alleged fact. The stars are not a celestial ballet, nor even a celestial game of billiards . . . All grounds for asserting this . . . went out with Ptolemy's system of astronomy' (Farrer, 277).

Nowadays it is biology, rather than astronomy, that is called in aid by the argument from design. Most notoriously, Teilhard de Chardin, with qualified but enthusiastic support from Sir Julian Huxley, has argued that evolution has a direction, a tendency to produce organisms of ever greater complexity and ever higher consciousness, which is the key to the (past and future) history of the universe. Sir Peter Medawar, on the other hand, says firmly 'The idea that evolution has a main track or privileged axis is unsupported by scientific evidence' (Medawar, 77).

---

tionem, non ab aliquo agente intendente finem, sed ab eo quod est per se vanum, id est a casu. Quaecumque vero non habuerunt talem dispositionem sunt destructa, et quotidie destruuntur; sicut Empedocles dixit a principio fuisse quosdam generatos, qui ex una parte erant boves, et ex alia parte erant homines (*In Phys.* II, 253).

Whether there is a privileged axis of evolution seems to be partly a scientific question and partly a philosophical one. Let us try to isolate the philosophical element. Suppose that the evidence were such as to suggest that the outcome of the process of evolution as a whole had been favourable to organisms of a certain kind: would it be possible to regard the universe as a system whose goal was to produce such organisms?

If systems are defined by contrast with their environment, it seems difficult to regard the universe as a system at all, since it has no environment. This problem, first clearly stated by Hume, has recently been eloquently restated by Professor Flew. Flew quoted Aquinas' statement of the argument from design in ScG I, 42. 'The arrangement of diverse things cannot be dictated by their own private and divergent natures; of themselves they are diverse and exhibit no tendency to form a pattern. It follows that the order of many among themselves is either a matter of chance or must be attributed to one first planner who has a purpose in mind.' Flew asks how Aquinas knows that the elements 'of themselves . . . exhibit no tendency to form a pattern'. 'To know what tendencies' says Flew 'they possessed "in themselves" as opposed to knowing what they do and will do under various universal conditions, you would presumably have to be able to study them: either separated from the universe, which is manifestly senseless; and/or without any divine control, which is a notion which the theist himself would want to rule out' (Flew, 71).

It may be granted that if the argument from design goes: 'All universes exhibiting order have been designed; this is a universe exhibiting order; therefore this universe has been designed', no one but a madman would say that the first premise was an inductive generalization based on observation of universes. But Aquinas does not need either to claim to have observed other universes or to have observed the elements free from a universe or divine control. By observing 'what they will do under various universal conditions' he can distinguish between the things they do because the universal conditions are thus and such, and the things they would do in any universal conditions in which they existed at all. In doing this he is no more claiming to have observed anything extra-universal than Galileo in framing his laws of motion was claiming to have observed a frictionless body.

In fact, the connection between intelligence on the one hand, and the adaptation of means to end on the other, does not seem to be a simple empirical correlation at all:[1] the ability to make such adaptation appears to be one of the criteria for intelligence. One way, for instance, in which we would try to see whether Martians were intelligent would be looking for machines made by them. Flew might say that we would only know that things we found on Mars were machines, because we knew by induction the properties of the metals of which the machine were made, and knew they could not have become thus and so naturally. The following problem would then present itself. If, in a strange environment, we come across a system which appears to pursue goals which could not have been predicted from a fortuitous conglomeration of the elements composing it, how do we know when we are facing a simple form of life, and how do we know when we are facing an artefact produced by a more developed, intelligent being? One factor in such a decision seems to be knowledge of the goals of the postulated intelligent being: certainly in the case of human artefacts we are unfamiliar with (for instance, discoveries among the earlier civilizations), we know they are artefacts partly because we know what human ends they would serve. To the extent that this is true, knowledge that a complex found on Mars was a machine would be posterior to knowing the goals of Martians. But this will not help the argument from design: for to know that the universe was designed would have to be posterior to knowing God's purposes. What use

---

[1] Flew himself is inclined to think that if it is not this, it must be a tautological definition, which it clearly is not. This is based on a positivistic dichotomy which many philosophers would reject independently of the merits of the present argument.

to anyone, we might ask, is this enormous parcel of galactic junk?

On the other hand, if the argument from design ever had any value, it has not been substantially affected by the scientific investigation of living organisms from Descartes through Darwin to the present day. If Descartes is correct in regarding the activities of animals as mechanistically explicable, then a system may operate teleologically while being mechanistic in structure. If Darwin is correct in ascribing the origin of species to natural selection, then the production of a teleological structure may be due in the first instance to factors which are purely mechanistic. But both may be right and yet the ultimate explanation of the phenomena be finalistic. The only argument refuted by Darwin would be one which said: wherever there is adaptation to environment we must see the immediate activity of an intelligent being. But the argument from design did not claim this; and indeed it was an essential step in the argument that lower animals and natural agents did not have minds. The argument was only that the ultimate explanation of such adaptation must be found in intelligence; and if the argument was correct, then any Darwinian success merely inserts an extra step between the phenomena to be explained and their ultimate explanation.

But was the argument ever valid? Granted that the adaptation of means to ends is a criterion for intelligence, can we say that wherever there is regular operation in a beneficial manner ere this adaptation of means to ends? It seems clear that we cannot; yet it is difficult to say what more is needed for the behaviour of a system to count as the selection of means to an end over and above its being regularly adaptable for the benefit of the system in question. This is an enormous, and unsolved, problem in the philosophy of mind; and a definitive verdict on the argument from design must wait on its solution.

Aquinas' own version of the argument, however, can be more briefly dealt with. For he seems to have sawn off the branch he was sitting on when, at *In Phys.* II, 259, he discussed the apparent intelligence of spiders and swallows. He says: 'it is obvious that they act by nature and not by intelligence because they always perform in the same manner: every swallow makes its nest in the same way, and every spider weaves its web like every other, which they would not do if they acted with intelligence and skill, since not every builder builds a house in the same manner'.[1] But if it is only irregular adaptive behaviour which calls for intelligence, then we do not need to look for any intelligence other than human, since only humans, according to Aquinas, exhibit irregular adaptive behaviour. On the other hand, if even regular adaptive behaviour calls for intelligence, Aquinas has given us no reason why we should not call the swallows and the spiders intelligent themselves, rather than looking for an intelligence to direct them from outside the universe.

Indeed it seems much easier to conceive of an intelligence incarnate in the body that exhibits the purposive behaviour than it is to conceive of a discarnate controlling intelligence. For in the case of the human beings and higher animals to whom we attribute degrees of intelligence, the adaptation of means to ends which is to be explained is, mediately or immediately, brought about by manipulation by the organisms in question. There are some who believe in psychokinesis, stretching the concept of intelligence in such a way that a human will is supposed to control events in the world without any intervention of the human body. There are serious difficulties in extending the concept in this way, and in particular it is not easy to interpret what is said of the act of the will which is supposed to cause the change in the world. But at least the experimental subjects can be given and take in orders such as 'will the six to turn up', and this gives a connection, however tenuous, between whatever takes place in

[1] ex hoc fit manifestum quod non operantur ex intellectu, sed per naturam, quia semper eodem modo operantur; omnis enim hirundo similiter facit nidum et omnes araneus similiter facit telam, quod non esset si ab intellectu et arte operarentur; non enim omnis aedificator similiter facit domum . . .

their minds and the normal exercise of the will in voluntary bodily activity. Moreover, the field in which the effects of this quasi-volition are alleged to occur, is limited by the terms of particular experiments: the fall of a particular set of dice, the turning up of cards from a given pack. The concept of intelligence has to be extended very much further if we are to speak of an intelligence whose normal mode of operation is not bodily at all, and whose field of operation is the whole of heaven and earth.

Bibliography

Bibliography

The scholastic literature on the Five Ways is extremely extensive. The reading list given below is very selective, with a bias towards works more likely to be intelligible to philosophers in the analytic tradition. The bibliography to each chapter includes only works expressly cited in the text.

General Reading List

Aquinas, T. *Summa contra Gentiles*, Marietti, 1946; Engl. trs. Pegis, Doubleday Image Paperback, New York, 1955.

Aquinas, T. *Summa Theologiae*, Marietti, 1952; Eng. Trans. of Ia, 2–11, Macdermott, London, Blackfriars, 1964.

Doctor Communis 7 (1954) *Sulle cinque vie di S. Tomasso.*

Doctor Communis 18–20 (1966) *De Deo in philosophia S. Thomae et in hodierna philosophia.*

Flew, A. *God and Philosophy*, London, Hutchinson, 1966.

Geach, P. 'Form and Existence', *Proceedings of the Aristotelian Society*, 1955.

Geach, P. 'Aquinas' in *Three Philosophers*, Oxford, Blackwell, 1961.

Gilson, E. *Elements of Christian Philosophy*, New York, Doubleday, 1960.

Mascall, E. *He Who Is*, London, Longmans, 1943.

Preller, V. *Divine Science and the Science of God*, Princeton, 1968.

Sillem, E. *Ways of Thinking about God*, London, Darton, Longman Todd, 1962.

Chapter One

Flew, A. and McIntyre, A. *New Essays in Philosophical Theology*, London, SCM, 1955.

Strawson, P. F. *The Bounds of Sense*, London, Methuen, 1966.

Williams, B. and Montefiore, A. *British Analytical Philosophy*, London, Routledge, 1966.

Chapter Two

Gilson, E. *Elements of Christian Philosophy*, New York, Doubleday, 1960.

Hoenen, P. *Cosmologia*, Rome, Pontificia Universitas Gregoriana, 1949.

Jammer, M. *Concepts of Space*, New York, Harper and Brothers, 1960.

Masi, R. 'De Prima Via' in *Doctor Communis* 18 (Vatican City, 1966).

Owens, J. C.S.S.R. (1) 'The conclusion of the prima via', *Modern Schoolman*, 30 (1952–3), 33ff.

(2) 'Aquinas and the proof from the Physics', *Medieval Studies*, 1966, 119–150.

Ross, W. D. *Aristotle's Physics*, Oxford, Clarendon Press, 1936.

Salamucha, J. 'The proof "ex motu" for the existence of God', *New Scholasticism*, 32 (1958), 327ff.

Sciama, D. W. *The Unity of the Universe*.

Vanni–Rovighi, S. 'La Prima Via Tomistica' in *Doctor Communis* 18.

Wallace, W. A. 'Newtonian antinomies against the Prima Via', *Thomist*, 19 (1956), 151–192.

Williams, C. J. F. 'Hic autem non est procedere in infinitum', *Mind*, 69 (1960), 403–405.

Chapter Three

Beth, E. W. *The Foundation of Mathematics*, North Holland, 1959.

Clark, Bowman L. 'Philosophical arguments for God's existence' *Sophia*, 3 (1964), 3ff.

Garrigou-Lagrange, R. 'La deuxième preuve de l'Existence de Dieu proposee par S. Thomas', *Doctor Communis* 7 (1954), 28ff.

McCabe, H. 'Causes' Appendix 2 in vol. 3 of the Blackfriars edition of the *Summa Theologiae*.

Preller, V. *Divine Science and the Science of God*, Princeton, 1968.

Salamucha, J. *art cit.* in ch. II.

Chapter Four

Anscombe, G. E. M. 'Hume Reconsidered', *Blackfriars*, 1962.

Finili, A. 'Recent work on the *Tertia Via*', *Dominican Studies*, 7 (1954).

Geach, P. and Anscombe, G. E. M. *Three Philosophers*, Blackwell, 1961.

Gonzalez Pola, O. P. 'El punto de partida de la tercerea via de Santo Tomaso', *Doctor Communis*, 19 (1966).

Hintikka, J. 'Necessity, Universality and Time in Aristotle', *Ajatus*, 20 (1957).

Hintikka, J. 'An Aristotelian dilemma', *Ajatus* 22 (1959).

Hoyle, F. *The Nature of the Universe*, Penguin, 1963.

Jalbert, G. *Necessité et contingence chez S. Thomas D'Aquin et ses prédecesseurs*, Ottawa, 1961.

Kenny, A. 'Necessary Being', *Sophia*, I (1962).

Pattin, A. 'La structure de la Tertia Via', *Doctor Communis*, 18 (1965), 253–258.

Prior, A. *Formal Logic*, Oxford, University Press, 1955.

Williams, C. J. F. 'Aristotle and Corruptibility', *Religious Studies* 1, 95–107.

Chapter Five

Allen, R. E. (ed.) *Studies in Plato's Metaphysics*, London, Routledge, 1965.

Bambrough, R. *New Essays on Plato and Aristotle*, London, Routledge, 1965.

Geach, P. (1) 'Form and Existence', *Proceedings of the Aristotelian Society*, 1955.
        (2) 'The Third Man again', in Allen.
        (3) *Three Philosophers*, Blackwell, 1961.

Gilson, E. *Elements of Christian Philosophy*, New York, Doubleday.

Owen, G. E. L. 'Aristotle on the snares of ontology', in Bambrough.

Quine, W. V. O. (1) *From a Logical Point of View*, Harvard, 1961.
        (2) *Word and Object*, M.I.T., 1960.

Vlastos, G. 'Degrees of Reality in Plato', in Bambrough.

Chapter Six

Ayer, A. J. *Philosophical Essays*, London, Macmillan, 1954.

Farrer, A. *Finite and Infinite*, London, Dacre Press, 1943.

Flew, A. *God and Philosophy*, London, Hutchinson, 1966.

Kenny, A. *Action, Emotion and Will*, London, Routledge, 1963.

Klubertauz, G. P. 'St. Thomas' treatment of the axiom omne agens agit propter finem' in *An Etienne Gilson Tribute* (C. J. O'Neil ed.), Milwaukee, 1959.

Medawar, P. *The Art of the Soluble*, London, Methuen, 1967.

Noble, D. (1) 'Charles Taylor on teleological explanation', *Analysis*, 27 (1967), 96–103.

     (2) 'The conceptualist view of teleology', *Analysis*, 28 (1968), 62–63.

Taylor, C. (1) *The Explanation of Behaviour*, London, Routledge, 1964.

     (2) 'Teleological explanation', *Analysis*, 27 (1967), 141–5.

Index

Index